Tribunal

Tribunal

A Courtly Comedy in Three Acts

Vladimir Voinovich

translated with introduction
and notes by Eric D. Meyer

ANTHEM PRESS

Anthem Press
An imprint of Wimbledon Publishing Company
www.anthempress.com

This edition first published in UK and USA 2022
by ANTHEM PRESS
75–76 Blackfriars Road, London SE1 8HA, UK
or PO Box 9779, London SW19 7ZG, UK
and
244 Madison Ave #116, New York, NY 10016, USA

First published in the UK and USA by Anthem Press in 2021

Original title: Tribunal: A Courtly Comedy in Three Acts

Copyright © Vladimir Voinovich 2022

Originally published by Overseas Publications Interchange Ltd, 1985
English translation and Introduction copyright © Eric D. Meyer 2021
The moral right of the authors has been asserted.

All rights reserved. Without limiting the rights under copyright reserved above,
no part of this publication may be reproduced, stored or introduced into
a retrieval system, or transmitted, in any form or by any means
(electronic, mechanical, photocopying, recording or otherwise),
without the prior written permission of both the copyright
owner and the above publisher of this book.

British Library Cataloguing-in-Publication Data
A catalogue record for this book is available from the British Library.

ISBN-13: 978-1-83998-544-7 (Pbk)
ISBN-10: 1-83998-544-5 (Pbk)

Cover images: RVK Design, Domen Colja and wk1003mike / Shutterstock.com

This title is also available as an e-book.

CONTENTS

Introduction: Please Allow Me to Introduce ... Vladimir Voinovich's
    Tribunal and Soviet *Samizdat* Writing   1

Dramatis Personae   21

First Act   23

First Intermission   77

Second Act

Second Intermission   107

Third Act

Index of Names   123

INTRODUCTION: PLEASE ALLOW ME TO INTRODUCE ... VLADIMIR VOINOVICH'S *TRIBUNAL* AND SOVIET *SAMIZDAT* WRITING

i

What do twenty-first century American readers know about the twentieth-century Soviet Union? Probably very little, I'd guess. Two generations have passed since the fall of the Berlin Wall and the breakdown of the Soviet satellite-states in Eastern Europe (the so-called Warsaw Bloc), along with the dissolution of the Soviet Socialist States in the Baltics, the Balkans, and Central Asia, ended the Cold War superpower struggle between the United States and the USSR, which some, like Samuel Huntington and Frances Fukuyama, claimed the United States had won when the Soviet Union collapsed between 1989 and 1991.[1] And with the spectacularly anticlimactic passage of the Cold War era, Western (and especially American) interest in the Soviet Union decreased dramatically, making scholarly Sovietology an almost extinct academic discipline and placing the twentieth-century Soviet Union roughly on par, in the public mind, with the tenth-century Byzantine Empire.

After the chaos and confusion of the collapse of the Soviet Union, when Boris Yeltsin struggled, only partly successfully, to bring democracy to post-Soviet Russia, and finally sent the post-Soviet tanks against the Russian Parliament in 1993, a "New Russia" gradually emerged—Vladimir Putin's Russian Federation—that, superficially at least, bears little resemblance to the Stalinist Communist Soviet Union. And the glorious heyday of the Cold War, when Soviet political dissidents and Russian *samizdat*[2] writers served as political pawns for Western agents, and the United States and USSR carried on a feverish propaganda war for global hegemony, has faded from memory, along with obscure world historical events like the Stalinist Great Terror, the

Moscow show trials, the Cuban Missile Crisis, and Khrushchev's "We Will Bury You!" speech.

What do contemporary readers know about Vladimir Voinovich's *Tribunal*? Probably even less, I'd guess. Published only in an extremely limited edition by a Russian émigré publishing house in London in 1985, Voinovich's *Tribunal: A Courtly Comedy in Three Acts* has never gotten the attention of his major novels, like *The Life and Extraordinary Adventures of Private Ivan Chonkin*, or his critical essay collections, like *The Anti-Soviet Soviet Union*, that made him one of the most famous Soviet dissidents of the Cold War era. But maybe with the publication of an American English translation, even in this post–Cold War period, there is some hope that Voinovich's *Tribunal* might get the critical attention from English-speaking readers that it so richly deserves.

For contemporary readers unfamiliar with either the now-defunct Soviet Union or Soviet *samizdat* literature, Voinovich's *Tribunal* might be characterized as a comparatively minor work by a twentieth-century Russian writer of epic historical novels (the *Chonkin* trilogy, *Monumental Propaganda*) and wildly satirical send-ups (*The Fur Hat*, *The Raspberry Pelican*), who has sometimes been celebrated, whether extravagantly or not, as "Russia's greatest living satirist." But Voinovich's *Tribunal*, I would argue—and, after reading, the reader might agree—is really his most important work, eclipsing even his critically acclaimed satirical masterwork, *Moscow 2042*, in its scathing political satire and sarcastic social commentary, which targets not only the Soviet Communist party, with its Stalinist purges and Moscow show trials, but also the persecution—and the prosecution—of political dissidents and nonconformist writers everywhere. And although the Cold War superpower struggle between the United States and the USSR and the Soviet dissident trials that serve as the world historical backdrop to Voinovich's *Tribunal* may appear, to contemporary readers, to belong to the distant past (the 1960s and 1970s), post-Soviet persecution of political dissidents continues, in Putin's New Russia, with such spectacularly farcical events as Sergei Magnitsky's posthumous trial, when the defunct Magnitsky, who had died in a Russian prison under suspicious circumstances, was convicted, in absentia, of tax evasion; and the persecution and exile of Mikhail Khodorkovsky, who was tried by the Putin regime, like the 1960s Soviet dissidents, inside the bars of a cage, before being sent to a Siberian labor camp.[3]

Voinovich's *Tribunal: A Courtly Comedy in Three Acts* was first published by Overseas Publishing Interchange, in London in 1985. And it is this version of Voinovich's work, with additional revisions by the author, that is the basis of the present translation, which attempts to convey the satiric spirit of Voinovich's Cold War Soviet comedy to a post–Cold War, post-Soviet, English-speaking audience. Although certain satiric allusions in Voinovich's *Tribunal* may appear obscure to contemporary readers, sometimes requiring the translator's notes to make their pointed reference clear, contemporary readers will still, I think, find that Voinovich's satire is as relevant to the twenty-first century New Russia as it was to the twentieth-century Soviet Union. And they may also find that Voinovich's satire on the Old Soviet Union and its Stalinist bureaucracy is also just as relevant to twenty-first century America, where President Donald J. Trump's White House cabinet often appears as wildly surrealistic and farcically inept as something straight out of Voinovich's satiric works: from *Moscow 2042* to *Washington D.C. 2020*.[4]

ii

As for Voinovich's biography: Vladimir Nikolayevich Voinovich, born in Stalinabad (Dushanbe), Tajikistan, to a Serbian father and a Jewish mother on September 26, 1932, was a Soviet political dissident and New Russian writer whose career followed the trajectory of Russian cultural life in the 60-year period from the Stalinist Great Terror and World War II, through the death of Stalin in 1953 and the subsequent "thaw" (*ottepel*) of the 1960s and 1970s, through the Brezhnev-era "stagnation" (*zastoj*) of the 1980s, through the collapse of the Soviet Union between 1989 and 1991, and into the twenty-first century New Russia.[5] During that frequently stormy period, Voinovich documented the changes in the Soviet Union and New Russia in both essayistic prose (*The Anti-Soviet Soviet Union, The Ivankiad*) and satiric novels (*The Life and Extraordinary Adventures of Private Ivan Chonkin, Pretender to the Throne, Displaced Person, Monumental Propaganda*), and in political theater (*Tribunal*), often employing the Aesopian allegory used by Soviet dissidents and Russian *samizdat* writers to talk about controversial issues considered forbidden and taboo by the Soviet secret police and the New Russian censors. And although the discomforting era of the 1930s Great Terror and the 1960s/1970s Soviet dissident trials finally became a distant memory, and both Khrushchev and Brezhnev finally passed away (in 1971 and 1982, respectively), Voinovich continued to employ his Aesopian allegory to satirize Vladimir Putin and the twenty-first century New Russia in his recent works, *The Myrzik Factor* (2017) and *The Raspberry Pelican* (also 2017).[6]

Voinovich made his debut on the Soviet literary scene with the publication of the short story, "We Live Here," in 1961, at an especially propitious moment for Soviet dissident literature, when Alexander Tvardovsky's journal, *Novy Mir* ("New World"), was also publishing Vladimir Tendryakov's *The Trial* (1960–61) and Alexander Solzhenitsyn's *One Day in the Life of Ivan Denisovich* (1962). But Voinovich's first explicitly politically dissident novel, *The Life and Extraordinary Adventures of Private Ivan Chonkin*, while evidently already in progress at that time, was forbidden publication in the USSR and was only published, some years later, by foreign publishers in Frankfurt am Main (1969) and Paris (1975). But although many of Voinovich's works were forbidden publication in the Soviet Union and first published in *tamizdat* in the West, Voinovich never ceased satirizing Russian society, whether as a Soviet dissident-in-exile (between 1974 and 1990) or as a returned Russian citizen (from 1990 to his death in 2019), and he was the recipient of such celebrated prizes as the *State Prize of the Russian Federation* (2000) and the *Andrei Sakharov Prize for Writer's Civic Courage* (2002).

Throughout his tumultuous career, Voinovich remained a quintessentially Russian writer, even if his stubborn "Russianness" was frequently scathingly critical of the political propaganda of the Soviet authorities and their New Russian counterparts. As he himself once said, "I am a Russian writer. I write in Russian, on Russian topics and in the Russian spirit. I have a Russian worldview."[7] And despite the whirlwind changes in the Old Byzantine worldview that accompanied the political transition from the twentieth-century Soviet Union to the twenty-first century New Russia, Voinovich's satiric genius kept pace with those changes, when it was not, as becomes clear from reading *Tribunal*, several giant steps ahead of them. Voinovich, in fact, even rewrote a version of *Tribunal* for twenty-first century Russian (and American) audiences more familiar with *VK/Kontakte* (the Russian *Facebook*) and African American rap music than with Stalinist communism or *The Collected Writings of Marx and Engels*. But it is the twentieth-century version of *Tribunal* that is translated here, on the presumption that it will appear as strangely provocative, as outrageously sarcastic, and as wildly funny, to contemporary readers, as when it was first produced for the Russian émigré community in London, back in 1985.

iii

During the brief hiatus between Voinovich's earlier and later works—that is, between "We Live Here" (1961) and *Tribunal* (1985)—the Soviet writers Andrei Sinyavski (*The Trial Begins*, 1960) and Yuri Daniel (*This Is Moscow Speaking*, 1962) were arrested by the KGB for publishing forbidden literature and put on trial between February 10 and 14, 1966, in one of the most widely known Soviet dissident trials. The Sinyavski/Daniel trial immediately drew international attention from a worldwide audience of critics, intellectuals, and writers and brought pleas for their release by Nobel Prize winners and international celebrities like Gunter Grass, Grahame Greene, Francois Mauriac, Arthur Miller, and Ignacio Silone. Voinovich himself, in a petition signed by 62 other Moscow writers, suggested that Sinyavski and Daniel should be released to the custody of the Soviet writers' community,[8] a plea that was ignored by the Soviet authorities. But while Sinyavski and Daniel were sentenced to terms in the Soviet forced-labor camps (the Gulag), the Sinyavski/Daniel trial brought international criticism of Soviet political justice and helped to create the atmosphere in which Voinovich's *Tribunal* was written.

The Sinyavski/Daniel trial, by Voinovich's own confessions, had a strikingly dramatic effect on his life and writing. As he admitted,

> The event shook me. Up [un]til then, I had written rather critically of Soviet life, but at the same time I was completely loyal and apolitical. [...] Now I realized that events were happening that concerned me directly. Today Sinyavski and Daniel [were] on trial, and tomorrow they would try me for something or other or even for nothing at all.[9]

And after writing protest letters to the Soviet authorities in support of Sinyavski and Daniel, Voinovich found his situation greatly changed. "My plays[,] which had been running successfully in fifty theaters in the country, my film scripts [...] were banned. [...] Party propagandists disseminated all sorts of slander about me, right down to saying I was connected with foreign intelligence and was a smuggler."[10] Voinovich, like the satiric antihero of his play, Senya Podoplekov (aka "Sensky Suspectnikoff"), suddenly found himself facing secret police persecution and public ostracism as a man under suspicion by the Soviet authorities. But unlike his fictional antitype, the Suspectnikoff of *Tribunal*, Voinovich did not succumb to pressure from the KGB to become a political dissident and a writer-in-exile but, instead, continued to live and work, for the time being at least, in the 1970s Soviet Union.

But those were difficult times for Soviet political dissidents; and difficult times, too, for Voinovich. As he explained in an interview with American critics in 1984,

> Yes, they persecuted me, expelled me from the Writer's Union; my books were banned again, they badgered me [...] I was threatened with all sorts of punishments, my phone was disconnected, crowds of KGB men followed me around, but I behaved as I wanted to and wrote what I liked. I have sometimes been called a fighter for freedom, but [...] I wasn't fighting for freedom, I was enjoying it. And freedom is the greatest gift a man can possess.[11]

And, in the end, Voinovich, unlike Suspectnikoff, can be said to have won his struggle against the Soviet authorities—although not without the enormous cost in psychological trauma and emotional suffering recorded in his well-known essay collections, *The Ivankiad* and *The Anti-Soviet Soviet Union*, and in his perhaps less well-known but maybe more important play, *Tribunal: A Courtly Comedy in Three Acts*.

iv

During the Sinyavski/Daniel period, Voinovich was already circulating early drafts of *Chonkin* in *samizdat*, struggling with the Soviet authorities to get a two-room apartment for himself and his wife (as recorded in *The Ivankiad*), evading the inept attempts of the KGB to assassinate him with a poisoned cigarette (as described in "An Incident in the Metropole"),[12] and, in perhaps his most heroic act, working with Semyon Lipkin and Andrei Sakharov to smuggle a microfilmed copy of Vasily Grossman's epic World War II novel, *Life and Fate*, out of the USSR. Grossman's *Life and Fate*, which scrupulously describes the frightful political purges and terroristic criminal excesses of the Soviet Union from Stalin's Great Terror and the Soviet Gulag through the Great Patriot War (World War II), had been confiscated ("arrested") by the KGB in February 1961; and despite Grossman's pleas to Nikita Khrushchev and the Soviet Central Committee to return the manuscript, *Life and Fate* was banned from publication in the USSR in Grossman's lifetime. After being smuggled out of the Soviet Union, *Life and Fate* was finally published posthumously in Lausanne, Switzerland, in 1980.[13]

Voinovich himself was expelled from the Soviet Writer's Union in 1974, exiled from the Soviet Union in 1980, and denied Russian citizenship in 1981. In his order stripping Voinovich of Russian citizenship, the general secretary of the Communist Party, Leonid Brezhnev, wrote that Voinovich had "systematically taken part in activities hostile to the U.S.S.R. and [had] brought harm to the prestige of the U.S.S.R. by his activities." In a scathing response, Voinovich wrote back:

> I have not undermined the prestige of the Soviet government. The Soviet government, thanks to the efforts of its leaders and your personal contribution, has no prestige. Therefore, in all justice, you ought to revoke your own citizenship.[14]

After this scathing rebuke, Voinovich went into exile for the next 10 years (1981–90); and *Tribunal* was written during this period of exile, although the action of the play—the prosecution of the Russian engineer, Senya Podoplekov/Sensky Suspectnikoff, for crimes against the Soviet State before a Stalinist tribunal—really suggests the events of 20 years earlier, especially the Sinyavski/Daniel trial. Subsequently, though, Voinovich was reinstated to

Soviet citizenship by Mikhail Gorbachev in August 1990; he was awarded a State Prize by the Russian Federation in 2000; and he divided his time between Russian émigré life in Munich, Germany, and his return to post-Soviet Russia. Throughout this 50-year period, Voinovich maintained his stance as a political dissident and continued to publish satiric and critical novels that satirized both the Stalinist dictatorship of Leonid Brezhnev (c.1964–82) and Vladimir Putin's New Russian regime (1999–).[15]

V

Voinovich's *Tribunal*, then, might easily be read as an Aesopian allegory of the cultural situation in the Soviet Union between the Death of Stalin in 1953, the Khrushchev-era "thaw" of 1956 to 1962, and the subsequent crackdown on political dissent and cultural liberalization during the Brezhnev years, between 1964 and 1982. During these turbulent years, comparatively liberal periods of permissive political policy and cultural tolerance ("thaws") alternated with comparatively conservative, reactionary periods of persecution of political dissidents and censorship of literature ("freezes"), often marked by political show-trials and official denunciations of public enemies. In Aesopian allegory, there's stereotypically a fairly direct, one-to-one correspondence between the characters and events of the allegorical fiction—for example, Voinovich's *Tribunal*—and the characters and events to which they correspond in the "real" (read: political) world—that is, the surrealistic world of the 1930s Stalinist show-trials and the 1960s Soviet dissident trials—that allows the Aesopian allegory to pass beneath the notice of the official censors, while still speaking directly to a sympathetic audience of political dissidents. Voinovich's *Tribunal*, with its dizzying shifts of style and mood and abrupt oscillations between tragedy and comedy, effectively captures the turbulent climate of the declining and falling Soviet Union in the 1970s/1980s Brezhnev era, and speaks to those political dissidents and activists who helped to bring about, from the wreck and ruin of the Soviet Communist downfall, the emergence of the twenty-first century post-Soviet New Russia.[16]

But there may also be, in Aesopian allegory, a certain ambiguity of reference that allows the allegorical fiction to sustain multiple interpretations, to make diverse political points, and to refer to different events and to different persons in the shifting political climate in which it was written and received by sympathetic readers. Voinovich's *Tribunal* thus refers comparatively directly to the 1960s Soviet dissident trials— the Joseph Brodsky trial (1964), the Sinyavski/Daniel trial (1966), or the Galanskov/Ginzburg trial (1968)—through which Voinovich himself—like his fictional anti-hero, Senya Podoplekov (aka Sensky

Suspectnikoff)—became unwittingly involved in politically dissident activities and faced persecution in the Soviet Union (although, unlike his alter ego, Voinovich was not imprisoned or tried for those subversive activities). But the central character of Voinovich's *Tribunal*, Podoplekov/Suspectnikoff, is not a Soviet writer but a Russian engineer[17] and could scarcely be said to correspond directly to Andrei Sinyavski or Yuri Daniel (let alone to Voinovich himself). Instead, Podoplekov/Suspectnikoff might be said to represent "The Soviet Comic Everyman," or, "The Everyday Soviet Citizen," who becomes caught up in the staggering political disputes and predatory power struggles of the Soviet Communist Party and its Stalinist cultural ministries, and so becomes an unwitting scapegoat and an unsuspecting pawn of the 1970s/1980s Cold War Soviet culture wars (and their Western counterparts), of which he is only dimly aware.

But besides this ambiguity of reference, which forbids reading Voinovich's play in a straightforwardly allegorical style, the contemporary reader should also observe that Voinovich's *Tribunal* wasn't actually written during the 1960s Soviet dissident trials but was written some 20 years later, in the uncertain years following the death of Leonid Brezhnev in 1982, when Communist Party cultural policies and Soviet political doctrines were once again caught up in bitter disputes between the comparatively conservative authorities and the controversial liberal activists. This ideological dispute is reflected, in Voinovich's *Tribunal*, in the conflict between **The Chairman** and **The Prosecutor**, who represent the Stalinist Old Guard of the 1930s Great Terror and The Great Patriotic War (World War II), and **The Secretary** and **The Public Defender**, who stand in for the Westernized progressives and Communist Party liberals who, in the 1960s and 1970s, challenged the Old Guard to modernize Soviet cultural policies. More specifically, the conflict between **The Chairman**, who is senile, sickly, and dying, and **The Secretary**, who is young and ambitious, corresponds fairly directly to the political in-fighting between Leonid Brezhnev (1964–82), the Stalinist conservative, and his successor, Andrei Andropov (1982–84), the supposed pro-Western liberal, whose ascendancy to Soviet power initially raised hopes for a "thaw"—hopes that were quickly crushed when the new general secretary pursued cultural policies that were largely the same as those of his Stalinist predecessor.[18] Voinovich's satiric response to Brezhnev's *diktat* stripping him (Voinovich, not Brezhnev) of Soviet citizenship has already been cited; and when, in the 1980s, Brezhnev was replaced by Andropov, Voinovich was already hard at work, incorporating those political changes into his satiric masterpiece, *Moscow 2042*, and into his farcical tragicomedy, *Tribunal: A Courtly Comedy in Three Acts*.[19]

vi

Besides its Aesopian allegory, Voinovich's *Tribunal* also belongs to a classic genre that might be called "the courtly comedy" or "the tragic show-trial," dating back to Sophocles' *Oedipus Tyrannus*, Aristophanes' *Wasps*, and Plato's *Defense of Socrates*. In this classic literary genre, the central character (Oedipus, Philocleon, Socrates, Podoplekov) is subjected to prosecutorial cross-examination by a hostile jury of politicians and citizens (the Greek chorus, the Athenian demes, the Soviet tribunal), whose blatantly criminal verdict is summarily dictated by the dizzily wavering scales of political injustice as they veer uncertainly between tragedy and farce. Although all these works might be described as Aesopian allegories, in which semi-mythological folk tales and childish beast-fables are employed to critique the courtly follies and political foibles of the current (democratic or communist) regime, Voinovich's Aesopian allegory most closely resembles Aristophanes' Old Attic Comedy in its Rabelaisian carnivalesque ribaldry and Bakhtinian rustic humor, which exposes the decadence and corruption of the Soviet authorities or the Greek demagogues of its time, by contrasting their hypocrisy to the simple morality of the common people, whose only weapon against their superiors is sarcastic, caustic humor. But Voinovich is a distinctly twentieth-century Aristophanes, inescapably confronted with the horrific political crimes and murderous insanities of the Soviet police state and the Stalinist terror, as more seriously described in Alexander Solzhenitsyn's *The Gulag Archipelago* (p. 1973/1974) or Vasily Grossman's *Life and Fate* (p. 1980).

The Greek tragic drama or Old Attic comedy of Sophocles or Aristophanes, like Voinovich's tragicomic farce, is essentially modeled upon the spectacular public debates between competing political factions that were a characteristic feature of both Greek democracy and of Soviet communism; and the central characters of these Greek psycho-dramas and Russian tragi-comedies (Oedipus, Philocleon, Socrates, Podoplekov) appear as tragic scapegoats or satiric comic butts, who must face the persecution of the dominant political majority essentially alone, in tragically hubristic isolation, until they are either redeemed, like Philocleon, and released from their solitary cells, or else condemned and convicted, like Oedipus, and sentenced to suffer cathartic expiation for the whole tragic community. In Greek classic tragedy, by Aristotle's famous theory in the *Poetics* (1449b21-28), the tragic hero's sufferings finally succeed in bringing about a cathartic purge and a redemption of the tragic community. But in Voinovich's *Tribunal*—as in, say, Aristophanes' *Wasps*—there is no catharsis-by-suffering of the tragic protagonist and no salvation of the tragic community, only a bewildering descent into sinister accusations and farcically insane plots, resulting in a tragicomic ending, in which the conviction of Podoplekov by this madcap Soviet tribunal is left very much in doubt.

But if Senya Podoplekov—whose Russian patronymic means something like "man under suspicion," or, "suspect with hidden motives"— is a Sophoclean Oedipus-figure or Platonic Socrates who suffers scathing cross-examination and scurrilous character-assassination throughout this spectacular public show-trial—and is subsequently (perhaps?) redeemed by his essential innocence—still, Podoplekov/Suspectnikoff, unlike Oedipus, never condemns himself or confesses to the fabricated crimes he's accused of by **The Prosecutor**, **The Public Defender**, and by the submachine-gun-toting secret policemen, **Gorelkin** and **Yurchenko**. Nor does he, like Socrates, present an eloquent, tightly argued plea in his own self-defense against the fabricated charges of this sinister tribunal. Instead, like the Philocleon of Aristophanes' *Wasps* or the Socrates of *Clouds*, Podoplekov/Suspectnikoff persists in his sporadic, spasmodic rebellions and slapstick comic protests against his stunningly inept accusers throughout this courtly comedic farce, until he is finally dragged offstage in a cage by the secret police, still protesting his innocence, in the spectacular final scenes of Voinovich's *Tribunal*.

But is **Suspectnikoff** to be admired for his heroic posturing? Or has he simply submitted to the pressures of the Western broadcast media to play the stereotyped role of **The Soviet Dissident**, who then becomes an unwitting pawn in the sinister spy-games and secret machinations of the Cold War superpower standoff between the United States and the USSR? The staggering climax of this absurdist melodrama leaves these troubling questions suspended without imposing a final moral on the audience, as **Suspectnikoff** is dragged offstage, and the stage-curtain falls on the whole motley crew of suspicious characters (and the no-longer-innocent spectators) of *Tribunal: A Courtly Comedy in Three Acts*. This sensational ending, while dramatically satisfying, is still highly problematic and morally ambiguous, and leaves the final verdict of the Soviet mock-justice tribunal as to the fate of Podoplekov/Suspectnikoff suspended between guilt and innocence, dizzily wavering in the wobbly scales of **Themis**, the Goddess of Justice, whose Greek statue presides over Voinovich's *Tribunal*. But Podoplekov's fate, rather than a judgment on himself, becomes a scathing indictment of the Soviet criminal justice system that condemns an innocent man to cruel and unjust punishment for crimes he did not wittingly commit, and so also condemns itself to the catastrophic decline and fall that would come to pass, a few years after the publication of Voinovich's *Tribunal* in 1985, with the collapse of the Soviet Union and the Soviet empire between 1989 and 1991.

vii

As might be expected, the Soviet Communist party and its Stalinist cultural policies spawned a whole spate of these courtly comedies or tragicomic show-trials in the politically fraught, litigious period between Stalin's Great Terror and the Moscow show-trials of the 1930s, the Doctor's Conspiracy after Stalin's death in the early 1950s, and the Sinyavski/Daniel trial of the mid-1960s. But although Voinovich's *Tribunal* might be placed in a distinctive literary genre with Andrei Sinyavski's *The Trial Begins* or Vladimir Tendryakov's *The Trial*, Voinovich's *Tribunal* also differs from its more sober, serious contemporaries in its wildly satirical style and burlesque, absurdist humor, which deflate the pretentious seriousness and pompous ceremony of the Stalinist show-trials and Soviet dissident trials more by satiric laughter and by raucous humor than by intellectual critique. For example, when Senya Podoplekov (aka **Sensky Suspectnikoff**) first figures out he's fallen into the trap of this sinister, prosecutorial tribunal, he pleads with his wife, Larissa (**Larissa Suspectnikova**): "Don't wait for me, Lara. Get married again. You're still young and beautiful, and your salary's not bad, either." And when Lara demurs, urging Senya to remember his children and family, asking: "What am I going to tell the children?" Podoplekov/Suspectnikoff replies: "Tell them ... Say, I got hit by a bus."

And immediately after this cloyingly intimate conversation, **The Chairman** of the Soviet tribunal, who's been listening in on the **Suspectnikoffs** from a secret coign of vantage in the W.C. where he's been hiding, peeks out from the stall-door and asks the Secretary:

> **Chairman** (*looking out of the restroom, checking out his clothes, signaling with his fingers to the Secretary, whispering*): Listen, Comrade Secretary. Is my ass showing?
> **Secretary**: Yes, Comrade Chairman.
> **Chairman** (*astounded*): Yass? And where else would we see the You, Ass, Ass, Are? What stupidity! I'm surrounded by asses! (*Slams the door.*)

And with this Rabelaisian touch, Voinovich debunks the Stalinist regime of the Brezhnev/Andropov period and deflates the tragic seriousness of the Soviet dissident trials, which are both, in his estimation, no more sophisticated than the wild beasts of Aristophanes' Aesopian allegories, no more dignified than the motley clowns of Italian Renaissance *comedia dell'arte* and no more to be taken seriously than the baggy-pants vaudevillains (sic) and red-faced clowns that might be found in an American three-ring circus or a borsch-belt comedy routine. Except that these buffoons and clowns are the Stalinist bureaucrats and Communist Party officials who preside over the gross miscarriage of Soviet criminal justice that is the satiric subject of Voinovich's *Tribunal*.

viii

But if Voinovich's *Tribunal* really is a scathing indictment of the Stalinist Communist regime and the Soviet criminal justice system for the sheer prosecutorial furor with which they pursued the 1960s Soviet dissident trials, at the expense of totally destroying innocent human lives, and, on the other hand, a self-righteous defense of the Soviet political dissidents who faced those criminal tribunals for the sheer moral courage with which they defended freedom of expression and civil and human rights ... Why, oh why, then? is Voinovich's ostensible protagonist, Podoplekov/Suspectnikoff, most definitely *not* a shining example of impassioned political dissidence and Socratic moral virtue as a strictly moralistic reading of Voinovich's *Tribunal* suggests, by rights, he should be? But, instead, Podoplekov/Suspectnikoff is a somewhat clumsy, buffoonish anti-hero and satiric comic butt, who fumbles and bungles his way through his prescribed role as a Cold War political scapegoat and an unwitting dupe of its sinister spy-games, without a great deal of either pride or dignity, and achieves the spectacular high point of his politically dissident career at the cost of the betrayal of his wife, his children, and his principles and the self-destruction of his own moral character as a self-respecting human being. And why is the tragicomic ending of this classically structured play so politically problematic and morally ambiguous? To the point that this spectacular ending also destroys whatever message or moral that might be extracted from Voinovich's Aesopian allegory?

> **Suspectnikoff** *(as he's dragged away, rattling the bars of the cage with his hands)*: I'll go on fighting to the end! It's better to die standing on your feet than to live on your knees! I declare a hunger strike! Alert the American President! Tell him Suspectnikoff's dying, but he still won't surrender! Alert the British Prime Minister! Alert the German Chancellor! Alert the Japanese Emperor! The Dalai Lama! The Pope in Rome! And all the progressive people of the whole world!
>
> **Cries from the Crowd**: Cut the lights!
>
> —Call the police!
>
> *The lights are extinguished. Shrill police whistles shriek. The sound of sirens grows louder, automobile tires hum, there's the noise of struggles, blue police-lights flash.*

Finally, the noise slowly dies away. And in the darkness, the clear, quiet voice of the **Bard** *is heard:*

—Why do flowers grow?
A child wanted to know.
The little flower answered:
—Only flowers know!
—But is there any use for flowers
If they just blossom and blow?
—Of course there is!
   The little flower answered [...]

And on this somewhat disturbing but pathetically tragicomic note, the lights go out on Podoplekov/Suspectnikoff and on the whole cast of Voinovich's *Tribunal*.

ix

Although clueing the spectators in, any further than this, on Voinovich's farcical plot might give away the sardonic punch-lines and stifle the groans and laughter, perhaps this much more might be said, by way of introduction, without entirely spoiling the fun: As the curtains open, the central characters, Senya Podoplekov (aka **Sensky Suspectnikoff**) and his wife Larissa Podoplekova (aka **Larissa Suspectnikova**), still clutching their free front-row tickets as they enter the sinisterly darkened, silent theater, walk into what they imagine to be a contemporary absurdist stage-play or surrealistic theatrical spectacle, only to discover they have become the unwitting guests-of-honor at a Soviet show-trial, whose picaresque, wacky humor and ribald, comic antics do not quite disguise the staggeringly tragic fate that awaits both the suspect characters and the unsuspecting audience of Voinovich's *Tribunal: A Courtly Comedy in Three Acts*.

Appendix to the Introduction: Voinovich's Brief Autobiography

I was born in 1932. I've lived in many different countries and in many different directions. I've worked as a shepherd, a carpenter, a sheet-metal worker, a district commissioner, a national radio editor, and a Princeton University professor. For four years I was a soldier for the Soviet Army. I finished five classes in public school: first, fourth, sixth, seventh, and tenth. For a whole year I taught in a children's school. In 1974, I was expelled from the Soviet Writer's

Union, in 1980 expelled from the USSR; and in 1981 lost my citizenship. Now I've been reinstated to citizenship, and I live in Moscow, in Munich, and in an airplane crossing between these two spots on the map.[20]

—from *Zamysel: Kniga* (1992)

Postscript: Voinovich's Obituary

While negotiations were still in progress for publication of this translation, Vladimir Voinovich died of a heart attack in Moscow on July 27, 2018. He had had two previous heart attacks. He was awarded obituaries in *The Washington Post* and *The New York Times* and on *Radio Free Europe/Radio Liberty*. He was preceded in death by his first wife Valentina Vasilievna Bolthushkina (1988) and his second wife, Irina Danilovna Braude (2004), along with a daughter from his first marriage, Marina Voinovich (2006), and a son from his first marriage, Pavel Voinovich (2018). His survivors include his third wife, Svetlana Y. Kolesnichenko, and a daughter, Olga V. Voinovich, a German writer.

Upon Voinovich's death, the Soviet dissident Viktor Davidov, who was himself incarcerated during the Soviet dissident era in a Stalinist-style mental hospital and forced to take psychoactive drugs that attacked his memory for circulating *samizdat* copies of Alexander Solzhenitsyn's *The Gulag Archipelago*, wrote: "Two hours ago, Vladimir Voinovich died. Heart attack. Shock. There you are, grandmother, and a lunar eclipse with a full moon. Something tells me I won't be able to sleep tonight." His absence will be felt in the post-Soviet dissident world of Putin's New Russia, where he was a still-satiric voice against censorship and brutality amidst the madness. May he rest in peace.

Notes

1 See Samuel Huntington, "Democracy's Third Wave," *Journal of Democracy*, Vol. 2, No. 2 (1991): 12–34; Frances Fukuyama, "The End of History," *National Interest*, 16 (Summer 1989): 3–18.

2 "'Samizdat' (from Russian, meaning 'self-published') is a [Russian] word that describes dissident activity across the Soviet bloc in which individuals reproduced censored publications by hand and passed the documents from reader to reader. 'Tamizdat' ('published over there') refers to literature and artwork, produced within the Soviet Bloc, but published abroad, often from smuggled manuscripts and masters." Definition by tamizdat artistic services at http://www.tamizdat.org/whoweare.html. By this definition, much of Vladimir Voinovich's early work qualifies as *samizdat* or *tamizdat* literature, but not *Tribunal*, which was written in exile and published and produced in Great Britain in 1985.

3 Sergei Magnitsky was a Russian lawyer and whistleblower who "uncovered a $230 million [...] tax fraud scheme run by a host of Russian interior ministry and

tax officials" and "was charged with running the fraud [himself] [...] Magnitsky was thrown into one of Russia's harshest pre-trial detention facilities, repeatedly denied medical care[,] and allowed to die" by his jailors. Despite his death, a Moscow court found him guilty of tax evasion anyway. In a stunning display of New Russian justice, "Magnitsky was spared a posthumous jail sentence after a Moscow judge acknowledged that he was already dead." See "Sergei Magnitsky Verdict 'Most Shameful Moment since Stalin'," *The Guardian*, July 11, 2013, archived at https://www.theguardian.com/world/2013/jul/11/sergei-magnitsky-russia-trial-verdict-tax-fraud. Mikhail Khodorkovsky, "once Russia's richest man, was jailed for eight years on fraud and tax evasion charges in a case widely seen as having political overtones after he [...] publicly clashed with President Vladimir Putin." During his trial, he appeared in a cage; and after his conviction, he was sent to a Siberian prison camp near a Soviet-era uranium mine, from which, it was reputed, few returned alive. He has since been released and gone into exile in the West. See "Khodorkovsky Trial Unfair, Human Rights Court Finds," *Financial Times*, July 25, 2013, archived at https://www.ft.com/content/0cc70c64-f50a-11e2-94e9-00144feabdc0; Masha Gessen, "The Wrath of Putin," *Vanity Fair*, April 2012, archived at https://www.vanityfair.com/news/politics/2012/04/vladimir-putin-mikhail-khodorkovsky-russia.

4 See Cathy Young, "Has Trump Destroyed Satire? Lessons from a Russian Dissident," *Forward*, October 25, 2017, archived at https://forward.com/opinion/386082/has-trump-destroyed-satire-lessons-from-a-russian-dissident/.

5 It should be mentioned that during the Great Terror, in 1936, Voinovich's father was arrested on charges of anti-Soviet agitation and sentenced to five years in the Stalinist labor camps (the Gulag). For Voinovich's biography, see Viktor Davidoff, "Voinovich and his Moral Compass," *Moscow Times*, July 30, 2018, archived at https://www.themoscowtimes.com/2018/07/30/vladimir-voinovich-and-his-moral-compass-a62380; Cathy Young, "The Life and Extraordinary Satires of Vladimir Voinovich," *Washington Examiner*, April 19, 2020, archived at https://www.washingtonexaminer.com/weekly-standard/russian-satirist-vladimir-voinovich-1932–2018; and "Russian Author, Former Soviet Dissident, Voinovich Dies at 85," *Radio Free Europe/Radio Liberty*, July 28, 2018, archived at https://www.rferl.org/a/russia-soviet-author-dissident-voinovich-dies/29395188.html.

6 For an excerpt of Voinovich's recent work in translation, see Cathy Young, "The Crimson Pelican," by Vladimir Voinovich, archived at https://medium.com/@CathyYoung63/the-crimson-pelican-ebc5c9d78396.

7 Vladimir Voinovich, *Conversations in Exile: Russian Writers Abroad*, ed. John Glad (Durham: Duke University Press, 1993): 97. For recent updates of Vladimir Voinovich's scathing comments on the current political situation, see, e.g., "Interview: At 80, Russian Writer Vladimir Voinovich still Builds Optimism on a Foundation of Pessimism," *Radio Free Europe/Radio Liberty*, September 26, 2012, archived at https://www.rferl.org/a/interview-vladimir-voinovich-80th-birthday/24720812.html; Cathy Young, "Prophet of Ukraine: The Russian Novelist Who's Seen It All Coming," *Weekly Standard*, Vol. 19, No. 31 (April 28, 2014), archived at https://www.weeklystandard.com/cathy-young/prophet-of-ukraine; and "Nearing 85, Russian Writer Urges Russia to Stop Looking Backwards," *Radio Free Europe/Radio Liberty*, August 9, 2017, archived at https://www.rferl.org/a/voinovich-85-russia-looking-backward/28667664.html. It should also be mentioned that Voinovich is of Serbian and Jewish ancestry, and has

spoken of his experiences as a Soviet Jew in an interview with Tatiana Bek, archived at https://lechaim.ru/ARHIV/151/bek.htm.
8   See Rosalind J. Marsh, *Soviet Fiction since Stalin* (London: Croom Helm, 1986), 15.
9   Vladimir Voinovich, "*Voinovich o sebe*," in *The Third Wave: Russian Literature in Emigration*, ed. O. Matich and M. Helm (Ann Arbor, MI: Ardis, 1984): 140. Translated in Robert Porter, *Four Contemporary Russian Writers* (Oxford: Berg, 1989): 92. Voinovich's description of Soviet political justice here echoes that of the Russian poetess, Anna Akhmatova, as cited by Nadezdha Mandelstam:

> We never asked, on hearing about the latest arrest, "What was he arrested for?"; but we were exceptional. Most people, crazed by fear, asked this question just to give themselves a little hope. If others were arrested for some reason, then they wouldn't be arrested, because they hadn't done anything wrong. They vied with each other in thinking up ingenious reasons to justify each arrest […] This was why we had outlawed the question: "What was he arrested for?" "What for?" Akhmatova would cry indignantly whenever, infected by the prevailing climate, anyone of our circle asked this question. "What do you mean, what for? It's time you understood that people are arrested *for nothing!*"

Nadezdha Mandelstam, *Hope against Hope*, trans. Max Hayward (New York: Atheneum, 1970): 11.
10 Voinovich, "*Voinovich o sebe*," 142–43; Porter, *Four Contemporary Russian Writers*, 93.
11 Voinovich, "*Voinovich o sebe*," 145. Porter, *Four Contemporary Russian Writers*, 95–96.
12 Because of the international scandal caused by the Sinyavski-Daniel trial, after 1966 the Soviet authorities displayed greater sophistication in their treatment of errant writers. They increasingly used the methods of deportation (in the case of Solzhenitsyn) or severe harassment (in the case of Voinovich) designed to force dissident writers to emigrate. After Voinovich had signed the letter protesting against the Galanskov-Ginsburg trial of 1968 there was a ban on the publication of his works for several years; and his *Ivankiad* graphically describes how in the 1970s the authorities cut off his phone and tried to force him to give up his flat to General Ivanko, a KGB official in the Union of Writers; in May 1975 he was even given a poisoned cigarette by KGB men in the Metropol hotel. Eventually he decided to emigrate [to Munich, Germany] for the sake of his own health and that of his family.

Marsh, *Soviet Fiction since Stalin*, 283.
13 Voinovich talks about Vasily Grossman's *Life and Fate* in the essay, "The Life and Fate of Vasily Grossman and His *Life and Fate*," in *The Anti-Soviet Soviet Union*, trans. Richard Lourie (New York: Harcourt, Brace & Jovanovich, 1985), 220–25. But, interestingly, he doesn't mention his role in smuggling the forbidden manuscript out of Russia.
14 Archived at http://www.sovlit.net/Voinovich.html from www.voinovich.ru.
15 It should also be observed, however, that Voinovich doesn't consider himself a political dissident, per se, but instead simply a satiric Russian writer.

> I have often said I do not consider myself a dissident, although by all the formal indicators I was. I wouldn't say I acted to defend human rights as a whole since I limited myself to defending the rights of just a few individuals. Besides

that, I was published abroad. Most important, whenever they threatened me, I would take up the challenge, and that was always a source of some pleasure. In fact, it was the authorities themselves who were to blame. I'm not in favor of smashing the state. Everybody knows what would come of that [...] For that reason I do not consider myself a political dissident.

Cited in Voinovich, *Conversations in Exile*, 93.

16 Voinovich, like other post-Soviet writers, still has mixed feelings about the collapse of the Soviet Union. Alexander Zinoviev, for example, who was a Soviet political dissident, quickly became disillusioned with the political changes accompanying the fall of the Soviet regime and described the entire twentieth-century Communist episode, from rise to fall, as a "Russian tragedy." See *Russkaya tragediya (gibel ytopii)* (Moscow: Algorithm Press, 2002). It should then also be observed that, although Voinovich was an outspoken critic of the Soviet regime, he did not necessarily advocate its downfall. In an interview given in July 1987, for example, Voinovich insisted that "In order for [Soviet President Mikhail Gorbachev's] *perestroika* to be effective and irreversible, it must happen by degrees. [...] Freedom and openness means democratization—and for a people not used to democracy this can lead to chaos." Cited in Marcia DeSanctis, "Dispatches from Russia: An Interview with Vladimir Voinovich," *Washington Times*, January 24, 2013, archived at http://www.tinhouse.com/blog/22200.html.

17 In *The Gulag Archipelago*, Alexander Solzhenitsyn points out that Russian engineers were frequently imprisoned or purged by the Stalinist Communist authorities, not simply because of suspicions about their supposed "subversive" or "wrecking" activities, but because they were eminently useful to the Soviet Communist regime in its grandiose construction projects and military industrial ventures and could be kept readily accessible for slave labor in the Stalinist Gulag. See also Solzhenitsyn's *Cancer Ward*, Pt. 1 & 2, tr. Nicolas William Bethell, Baron Bethell, and David Burg (London: Bodley Head, 1968/1969). (This is the first edition English translation.)

18 As Rosalind J. Marsh observes, "Rumors that Andropov might be a liberal in cultural policy because of his liking for jazz and Western novels were soon scotched" when the new Soviet premier "advanced the traditional view that literature had the duty to help the party and state in its struggle for [law and] order." *Soviet Fiction Since Stalin*, 20. Cp. Voinovich's portrayal of "The Secretary" in Act II, scene 1, *et passim*.

19 As Voinovich describes the confused cultural climate of the Soviet 1980s,

> When Stalin was alive, most people could not imagine that he would ever die. Same under Brezhnev. [...] When I was leaving the Soviet Union [in 1980], I said that in about five years cardinal changes would begin. I didn't know what kind of changes; I didn't think the Soviet Union would collapse—I wasn't thinking in such terms. But I thought there would be drastic political changes. [...] I could also see that the KGB was assuming an increasingly important role in society. The country was being ruled by uneducated, incompetent people; they needed competent aides, and the KGB was a natural source. [...] The KGB elites were getting closer and closer to the men in power, and it was obvious that someday they would take power themselves and start to rule. In fact, even in those days, while I was writing the book [i.e., *Moscow 2042*], [Yuri] Andropov appeared on the scene—the KGB chairman who became the General Secretary—and then Putin came along. So, all these predictions—I

don't believe in parapsychologists or psychics, but I do believe that one can make logical deductions.

Cited in Cathy Young, "The Man Who Predicted Putin," in *The Daily Beast*, June 22, 2015, archived at https://www.thedailybeast.com/the-man-who-predicted-putin

20 Voinovich has also written an autobiography, currently untranslated, entitled *Self-Portrait: The Novel of My Life*. In Russian: *Автопортрет. Роман моей жизни* (Moscow: Эксмо, 2010).

A Short Bibliography

Works by Vladimir Voinovich

The Ivankiad, trans. David Lapega (New York: Farrar, Strauss & Giroux, 1976).
The Life and Extraordinary Adventures of Private Ivan Chonkin, trans. Richard Lourie (New York: Farrar, Strauss & Giroux, 1977).
In Plain Russian, trans. Richard Lourie (New York: Farrar, Strauss & Giroux, 1979).
Pytem vzoutou perepiski (Arcady: YMCA Press, 1979) (untranslated).
Pretender to the Throne: The Further Adventure of Private Ivan Chonkin, trans. Richard Lourie (New York: Farrar, Strauss & Giroux, 1981).
"Voinovich o cebe," in O. Matich and M. Helm, ed. *The Third Wave: Russian Literature in Emigration* (Ann Arbor, MI: Ardis, 1984), 137–42.
The Anti-Soviet Soviet Union, trans. Richard Lourie (New York: Harcourt, Brace, & Jovanovich, 1985).
Tribunal: sudebnaiā komediiā v trekh deĭstviiākh (London: Overseas Publications Interchange, 1985).
Moscow 2042, trans. Richard Lourie (San Diego: Harcourt Jovanovich, 1987).
The Fur Hat, trans. Richard Lourie (New York: Farrar, Strauss & Giroux, 1989).
Zamysel: Kniga (Moscow: Bagriys, 1992) (untranslated).
Monumental Propaganda, trans. Andrew Bromfield (New York: Alfred A. Knopf, 2004).
Avtoportet: Roman moei zhizni (autobiography) (Moscow: EKSMO, 2010) (untranslated).
A Displaced Person: The Later Life and Extraordinary Adventures of Private Ivan Chonkin, trans. Andrew Bromfield (Evanston, IL: Northwestern University Press, 2012).
Tribunal: Brachnaiā komediiā, sudebnaiā komediiā i vodevil' (play) (Moskva: EKSMO, 2014) (untranslated).
Faktor Murzika (novel) (Moscow: 'Э' Publishing, 2017) (untranslated).
Malinovyĭ pelican (novel) (Moscow: 'Э' Publishing, 2017) (untranslated).

Some Secondary Sources

Abram Tertz (Andrei Sinyavski), *The Trial Begins*, trans. Max Hayward (New York: Pantheon, 1960).
Leopold Labedz and Max Hayward, ed. *On Trial: The Case of Sinyavski (Tertz) and Daniel (Arzhak)* (London: Collins & Harvill, 1967).
Vladimir Tendryakov, *The Trial*, ed. Peter Doyle (Oxford: Basil Blackwell, 1990).
On Trial: The Soviet State versus "Abram Tertz" and "Nicholia Arzhak," revised edition by Max Hayward (New York: Harper & Row, 1967).
D. Alger et al., trans. Translated in *Three, Seven, Ace & Other Stories* (London: Harvill Press, 1973): 71–159.

O. Matich and M. Helm, ed. *The Third Wave: Russian Literature in Emigration* (Ann Arbor, MI: Ardis, 1984).
Clarence Brown, ed. *The Portable Twentieth Century Russian Reader* (New York: Penguin, 1985).
Joshua Rubenstein, *Soviet Dissidents* (Boston, MA: Beacon Press, 1985).
Vasily Grossman, *Life and Fate*, trans. Robert Chandler (New York: Harper & Row, 1985).
Rosalind J. Marsh, *Soviet Fiction Since Stalin* (London and Sydney: Croom Helm, 1986).
Robert Porter, *Four Contemporary Russian Writers* (Oxford: Berg, 1989).
Conversations in Exile: Russian Writers Abroad, ed. John Glad (Durham: Duke University Press, 1993).
John and Carol Garrard, *The Bones of Berdichev: The Life and Fate of Vasily Grossman* (New York: Free Press, 1996), esp. 321–22.

DRAMATIS PERSONAE

Sensky Suspectnikoff
Larissa Suspectnikova
The Chairman
The Prosecutor
The Public Defender
The Secretary
The First Juror
The Second Juror
The Bard
Gorelkin
Terrorekin
Greenskaya
Security Guards With Submachine Guns

    & **Two Clowns**, who also play various roles:

     Stage Worker
     Man With A Radio
     Spectators
     Poet
     Writer
     Scientist
     Secret Policeman Yurchenko
     Chicksa
     Hospital Attendants
     Demonstrators
     Foreign Correspondents

FIRST ACT

Act I, scene 1

*In the middle of the stage is a long, high table, covered with red cloth. Three chairs with high backs sit at the table. There are also three small tables: one in front of the big table in the proscenium, and two at the sides. A **Statue of Themis** stands in the background. Her eyes are blindfolded. In one hand, she holds a Kalashnikov; in the other, a pair of scales. On the scales are, in one pan, a hammer, and in the other, a sickle. On **Themis'** left is a cage, like those to hold wild beasts. In the cage is the defendant's bench. On the upper stage are wall-poster portraits of six people, for the present unknown to us.*

The Bard comes on stage with a guitar.[1] *He speaks quietly, in a homely, completely un-theatrical voice, in the empty spaces between playing phrases on the guitar.*

Bard: Sometimes I think they'll never get on with the show. The directors, I mean. The showmen. The producers. The executioners. For these guys, it seems to me, the script is never done. There's always something (*he fiddles with his fingers on the fretboard*) slightly out of tune. Even **The Chairman** never gets it right. He's getting old, he groans, he's got stenosis, sclerosis, adenoid troubles, but the doctors still fight for his health, just to keep him alive another day. Oh, all right. I'll play something for you, while we're waiting for the show to go on. (*He sings.*)

> The white river flows from far away
> And spills over field and meadow.
> The white river flows, and storm clouds blow
> This mad, mad world away.

The whole time he's playing, from somewhere offstage, at first far away and then getting closer, comes the frightful, broken sound of sirens, coming either from ambulances or from police-cars or from some other official machinery. As the sirens grow louder, **The Bard** *also plays louder, trying to outcry the sirens.*

> The sun beats down as the mad river flows,
> And the winter snows begin to cry.
> That's the way my whole life goes,
> Like a river falling into the sky…

Bard (*breaks off playing*): No, no, it's impossible. (*Pauses.*) I don't know why I have to do this, but…. (*Imitates the sirens.*) Ooo-ooo-ooo-oo… Whenever I hear that sound, it makes me want to put my hands up and reach for the sky. I think something bad must have happened to make them scream, like that. You see, I'm really no dissident. I'm really no fighter. If you want to know the truth, I'm against all kinds of fighting. Because nothing good ever comes from fighting. (*Hums.*) "And when you think you're fighting the good fight/You're only chasing a falling star." They promised you a sky full of diamonds. But, in the end, you only see stars. And when the fighting's over, the peace never lasts very long. So there's really no point in fighting. Just mind your own business and be thankful for what you've got, that's what I say….

The sound of the sirens grows louder. The stage-lights in the hall go out. The screaming of the sirens gets mixed up with the sound of enormous automobiles, rushing past at great speeds. From stage left and right, flashing blue lights swoop past, until the spectators become aware that a convoy has passed by. The blue flashes are extinguished and all sounds dissipate. What blue flashes stay lit on stage become completely dark. But suddenly, the stage-lights flare up, and, at the same time, from all aisles and doors, there appear **Security Guards With Submachine Guns** *who point their highly realistic weapons at the spectators.*

The Secretary *walks on stage in a plain dark suit. He struts in a business-like march to the stage's edge and stares intently at the public, as if he were trying to determine whether some suspicious persons were thinking bad thoughts. Finally, his doubts still un-assuaged, he withdraws behind the curtains. From loudspeakers hidden behind curtains comes thunderous applause, and in single file like a chorus line onto the stage come* **The Chairman**, **The Secretary**, **The Jurors**, **The Prosecutor**, *and* **The Public Defender**. *And now we see: It's their portraits that hang over the stage. All of them except* **The Secretary** *are older than their portrait. They are, generally, very old people. Carrying themselves with great dignity, they shuffle on their spindly old legs, but* **The Chairman** *keeps shaking his head with senility.* **The Party Members** *clap their hands, as if acknowledging the applause of a wildly enthusiastic public. Out of their hairy ears dangle the wires of their listening devices. They take their places on stage:* **The Chairman** *in the center,* **The Jurors** *at the sides,* **The Prosecutor** *at the small table to the left, and* **The Public Defender** *on the right with* **The Secretary**. *Silently they shuffle their*

court papers, sometimes whispering among themselves. Meanwhile, the public waits, waits… Finally, a woman in the front row can't stand the suspense any longer. She jumps up and starts pleading with her husband.
(*This is* **The Suspectnikoff Couple**.)

    Larissa: Senya, I don't understand what's going on here! Why are there so many people with guns?
    Suspectnikoff: Oh, calm down, Lara! Why are you so nervous? It's just a show!
    Larissa: I know it's just a show. But why are there so many people with guns?
    Suspectnikoff: Oh, I don't know why. Probably they need them for the show. Probably they're playing a role. Haven't you ever seen people with guns on stage before?
    Larissa: Sure, I've seen people with guns on stage before. But if this is a real performance, the actors should be saying something. But these guys are just standing there, playing dumb, not saying anything.
    Suspectnikoff: So what's to talk about? Maybe they're just acting, like they're in a silent movie. It looks like they must be playing some really important scene. (Addressing **The Chairman**.) Comrade artist. Can you tell us what role it is you're playing?

Some number of extras come onstage, adding to the confusion. **The Chairman** *exchanges glances with* **The Jurors**, *but they just shrug.* **The Secretary** *walks up to* **The Chairman**, *and, taking* **The Chairman**'s *earpiece, he starts whispering into it, like he's talking into a microphone.*

    Chairman: Ah, role! Role! (*To* **Suspectnikoff**.) I'm playing the role of **The Chairman of a Tribunal**.
    Suspectnikoff: There now, you see, Lara? I said this was just a show! And the comrade, just like he says, is playing the role of **The Chairman of a Tribunal**. (*To* **The Chairman**.) And so what else is happening? Are you getting this whole thing up, just so you can put on a show-trial?
    Chairman: Yes, you could say we're putting on a show-trial! But it's not just us who're putting on a show-trial. Because where there's a show-trial, you, know, it means we need somebody to try….
    Suspectnikoff (*to* **Lara**): Now, you see, Lara? I told you this was just a show! It's pretty catchy, I'd say, this clever plot! And where there's a show-trial, like they say, they need somebody to try. (*To* **The Chairman**) So will you put on this whole show-trial just like it's done

in Chekov?² You say, if you're putting on a show-trial, you need somebody to try. And so, if there's people with guns... Does that mean they'll need somebody to shoot? (*He laughs.*) Ha, ha! Get it? Gunmen? Need somebody to shoot?...

Prosecutor (*coming to life*): Bang, bang, bang! pow, pow! Just like in Chekov, right? Get it? Just like shooting a scene? Just like shooting a gun! Bang! bang! bang! pow! pow!

Chairman (*finally cutting off* **The Prosecutor** *and* **Suspectnikoff**): But have you really even actually read Chekov? Or just talked about reading him? Huh?

Suspectnikoff: Chekov? Well, of course I've read him! I'm a man of higher culture. There are, of course, people with diplomas who've never read anything much. But I always read everything in school. And I've even got a private library, a fairly mediocre one, but it's still not too bad, considering... It's true, though, of course, it's pretty hard to get good books, nowadays. They say it's because paper's scarce. And in the bookstores, there's just trash.

Larissa: Senya, why are you saying those things? You don't really know these people, and now you're saying all these things....

Suspectnikoff: What did I say, Lara? I didn't say anything, like that. I just said, there's nothing to buy. You walk into the bookstore, and there's maybe some of Brezhnev's speeches, Communist Party propaganda, Party Congress reports, reports about building kolkhozes, and so on and so forth. And maybe there's some foreign literary works, but still there's never enough good classic writers.³

Chairman: So you're interested in foreign literature, are you?

Suspectnikoff: Well, of course I'm interested in foreign literature! What do you think, for god's sake? I'm an intelligent, well-educated man. A man of culture, like I say, is what I am....

Chairman: For god's sake, did you say? Are you still a believer in gods?

Suspectnikoff: Me? Well, yeah, I guess you'd say... But I've never been baptized, see? So I'm not really a Christian. Okay, so, it's true, my father wanted me to be baptized. But I didn't go along with it, because I was a Young Communist. We lived in some small town, where there was just one church, and if you went to church, somebody might think you weren't happy with the Party line. But somehow, when I'd think too hard about what they got out of church... Well, sometimes some suspicious thoughts would slip into my mind. It's hard to explain... I'm sure you know, since you're **The Chairman**, but sometimes I'd see people, cows, dogs, all other kinds of animals, frogs and insects, and so on. And these strange thoughts would pop up out of the dust.

I'd think that, maybe somewhere, beyond all that stuff, there's must be some kind of higher intelligence.

Chairman: Do you still think there's something like that?

Suspectnikoff: Well, no, not really, I guess. That's just what I used to think, back when I was a kid, before I was re-educated. But still, from time to time, these doubts would spring up.

Prosecutor (*jerkily*): Bang! bang! bang! Pow, pow!

Chairman (*To The Prosecutor*): Did you want to say something?

Prosecutor: Yes, I just wanted to put a question to the citizen there. I heard you say that your father is a Party member. But you're not, you say?

Suspectnikoff: No. No, I'm not. I mean....

Prosecutor: But why not? What's wrong with you? You don't like the Party?

Suspectnikoff (*hurriedly*): Why not? What's not to like? The Party's good for us, and I subscribe to the Party line. And as for joining, well, I'm not, of course, opposed to it, because of course I want to do something to contribute to the Work, to do what's good for the Party... But I'm really not in good shape, it's something genetic, my mother and father were both slightly stunted in their growth, compared to the average... But still, in the attitude of service, they were nowhere without the Party. But, anyway, in my department, we just got some directive that says the Party has finally started to serve the working class. And that's good! That's great! That's fabulous! But, you see, where I work, the Engineering and Technical Department is divided into three working classes: machinists, watchmen, and boiler men. And, what's interesting is that the machinists are all alcoholics, the boiler men are just jailbait, but the watchmen are all Baptists, and so they won't join the Party, for religious reasons, you understand. So that's just how things stand in our party line. Like everybody, in Russia now, stands in line for something. Me, now, I stand in three lines. No, make that four lines: I stand in line for an apartment, I stand in line for a sports car, I stand in line for a Yugoslavian carpet, and I stand in line for the Communist Party.

Chairman: And do you think these things can go together? Your desire to join the Party, I mean, and your religious beliefs?

Suspectnikoff: What kind of beliefs have I got! Now, the watchmen, they have beliefs! And I think maybe there's something in our thinking that doesn't jibe. But if there's not, there's not. You know? To me, to tell the truth, it doesn't really matter. But excuse me, I'm detaining you. I'm just wasting your time. Don't you want somebody to try?

Chairman: What? Somebody to try? Why, we've got somebody to try! Like, for example, how about you?

Suspectnikoff: Who, me? Ha, ha! (*He laughs.*) Why me?

Chairman: And why not you?

Secretary: That's exactly it! Why not you, citizen?

Suspectnikoff: Because I'm really not like that, at all! I mean, I'm really just a simple man. An engineer. A nobody. I'm just like everybody else. I just want to go to work, come home, and watch TV. I watch hockey, figure skating, the *Time* program. And other than that, I never do anything much. I'm really no problem at all! (*Sits down on the bench.*) Really not a problem....

Chairman: But, Comrade Suspectnikoff. Every man who's alive is some kind of problem.

Secretary: Exactly, Comrade Chairman. Every man who's alive is some kind of problem. As Comrade Stalin used to say: Where there's a man, there's a problem. But if there's no man, there's no problem....[4]

Chairman: Now, what town did you say you're from? Speak up! And step right up here!

Secretary: And don't be shy!

Suspectnikoff (*embarrassed, standing up*): Who, me? But I'm just like you! (*Laughs.*) I really don't know how to act in front of the public! Because I'm really, like I say, not a performance artist.

Chairman: Oh yeah? And why are you not an artist? I'd say, you're an artist, already! Just step right up here! And take your place on public stage.

Suspectnikoff (*even more embarrassed*): But I'm really not like that! What kind of artist am I? If you need an assistant from the audience, you should pick somebody else. Because, in front of the public, I'm just terrified. I get stage-fright. Whenever the stage-lights strike me, I get stage-struck. And whenever I'm in front of a crowd, at a meeting or something, I just clam up. I can't go on. (*Pulling himself together.*) But if the show really must go on, you should go ahead and get started. Without me, you see. (*He sits down.*)

Chairman (*exchanging glances with **The Jurors**, laughing*): Oh, he's a funny guy, huh? A wise guy! A real clown! How could we get started without you? We're a tribunal, see? And so we need somebody to try! What on earth is a tribunal without somebody to try? Why, that's like a wedding without a bride! Like a funeral when nobody's died! Or a suspect with no place to hide... So just step up! Step up! already.

Secretary: Just be careful, you don't trip on the steps. You might hurt yourself.

Suspectnikoff (*jumping up*): Well, the hell with that! I thought you were just joking! I thought this was just a show-trial! But you guys want to make me some kind of dummy, or something! But I'm really not your puppet! I thought maybe you'd just strut around, put on a show-trial for me, and I'd just watch and go home. But if I went and complained to the management, and turned in my ticket, I wouldn't get my money back. So I stuck it out. But this is too much! already. (*To his wife.*) Come on, Lara. I don't want to watch this show-trial, anymore. It's just like I told you, this whole show-trial's nothing but show-trash!

Prosecutor: Bang! bang! bang! pow! pow!

Chairman (*To **The Prosecutor***): What's that? What'd you say?

Prosecutor (*getting upset, standing up*): Comrade Chairman. I look around me, at what's going on here, and I think: Aren't we being a little too humane? A little too liberal.

Chairman: Us? Humane? But, of course, we are humanists. Aren't we? Socialist humanists.

Prosecutor: Or socialist *anti*-humanists. But our humanism really shouldn't be quite so liberal or humane. Our socialist humanism should have something of a war-like, class-based character.[5] Like the class struggle. Like a class war. But what's going on here? You ask him something, politely. And he just insults you. He detains us and wastes the public's time. He insults our intelligence. But the public's waiting. And the show-trial must go on!

Suspectnikoff: You said it, comrade! The public's waiting! The public's always waiting for your socialist-realist work to get started! To do something for the working class. But you just keep going on with this stupid trash! You think this is something modern! Like, the theater of the absurd! You think, by some stupid trick, you can bring the audience on stage. Break down the fourth wall, like they say. But I think it's something obscene! And I don't want to watch this show-trial, anymore.

Larissa: I already told you, Senya. We don't have to play along with this show-trial.

Suspectnikoff: I already knew it was nonsense, Lara. But I just thought, with a title like "Tribunal," it might pass as a detective story. Or maybe a chiller thriller, with gangsters and spies, or something. But no-o! It's all just rubbish! Trash! Garbage! Stupid stage-tricks! C'mon, Lara. Let's get out of here.

Chairman: I'm telling you for the last time, citizen. Either you go along with us willingly, or we'll make you go along by force. I'm warning you, citizen, step up on the stage.

Suspectnikoff (*forcing his way toward the exits*): Now you think you can order me around! But I don't take orders from you! I'm getting out of here! Lara!
Chairman (*To the police*): Policemen! Bring him here!

The policemen blow their whistles. **Gorelkin** *and* **Yurchenko** *jump on stage, manhandling* **Suspectnikoff** *between them. A brief struggle ensues.*

Suspectnikoff (*resisting*): Get your hands off me! I'll make a complaint! Help me! People, help me! Don't you see what's happening here? Why are you playing dumb? Can't you see what's going on? Lara!
Larissa: Senya! They're hurting you!
Prosecutor: Comrade Chairman, I ask you to observe. He's resisting the police!
First Juror: He's attacking the police!
Second Juror: He's murdering the police!
Public Defender: What do you mean, murdering the police? He's not hurting them, and he's isn't even resisting arrest.

Act I, scene 2

Gorelkin *and* **Yurchenko** *drag* **Suspectnikoff** *onto the stage with his hands tied behind his back and start to strip-search him. They pull off his pea-jacket, turn his pockets inside out, and rip out the linings. They go through his pants pockets, pull off his belt, and cut off his trouser buttons. Finally, they yank off his shoes and remove his shoelaces.*[6]

Gorelkin (*following protocol, enumerating the items found in the search*): Soviet citizen's passport in the name of Sensky Vladilenovich Suspectnikoff, one. Trade union card, one. Theater tickets, two. Receipts for damages, two. *Prima* cigarettes, matches. One broken comb. One dirty handkerchief. One switchblade....
Public Defender: Why're you writing: "switchblade"? Why not just say "knife"?
Chairman: And what're you looking at, Gorelkin?
Gorelkin: Permit me to display to the court this black-eye, which I received during the suspect's arrest.
Prosecutor: I presume, Comrade Chairman, Gorelkin needs to report for a complete examination, to determine whether he's in immediate danger to his health, due to his serious injuries, you see.
Chairman: Good, good. Agreed. Gentlemen. You should familiarize yourself with the protocol for searches in these cases. Shackle the

arrestee to the defendant's bench and take Gorelkin to the appropriate institution. And now, if you'll excuse me....

He immediately falls asleep.

*The security guards drag **Suspectnikoff** into the wild beast cage, after which **Gorelkin** slips away, holding his hand over his eye, while **Yurchenko**, with a submachine gun, guards the wild beast cage. Inside the cage, **Suspectnikoff** sits at the defendant's bench, trying to calm down and assess the damages from the search. All the court officials stare blankly at **The Chairman**, but he just sits there snoring, oblivious. Finally, **The Secretary** approaches **The Chairman** and very cautiously shakes him awake.*

Secretary: Comrade Chairman! Comrade Chairman!

Chairman (*confusedly*): Ha? Wha'? Who're you?

Secretary: **The Secretary**, Comrade Chairman.

Chairman: What nonsense is this? How can you be the Comrade Chairman? That's me! I'm the Comrade Chairman! And so who are you?

Secretary: Okay! You're the Comrade Chairman! And I'm **The Secretary!**

Chairman: Ah, yes. That's right. **The Secretary.** Now, on to another case. What do we do next?

Secretary: We need to start the trial. The defendant's ready for questioning.

Chairman: The defendant? (*Blinks at **The Prosecutor**.*) But that, what's that there?

Prosecutor (*insulted*): Bang, bang, bang! pow! pow!

Secretary: No, no, Comrade Chairman. That's **The Prosecutor**. That's the defendant.

Chairman: Ah, yes. So it is. Now I remember. And is that the guy who shot Chekov?

Secretary: Comrade Chairman, that's not Chekov. That's a security guard.

Public Defender: Comrade Chairman, I protest these objectionable facts. My client didn't shoot the security guard. He just slapped him around, a little.

Prosecutor: What's the difference whether he slapped him or whether he shot him? It's obvious the policeman suffered a critical injury, and the doctors will testify he's struggling for his life.

Chairman: Stop this circus! Immediately! The show-trial must go on! (*Shaking himself awake. To **Suspectnikoff**.*) Defendant! Your name, patronymic and familiar.

Suspectnikoff: What's that? Were you talking to me?

Chairman: Of course I'm talking to you! Who else would I be talking to?

Suspectnikoff: But maybe I just don't call myself the defendant.

Chairman: It doesn't matter what you call yourself. Whether you call yourself the defendant, or not, is irrelevant! It only matters whether we call you the defendant.

Secretary: That's just it! It doesn't matter what you call yourself! It matters what *we* call you. Get it, now, defendant?

Chairman: Yes, and... Defendant, at this trial, when you're called before the court, you will rise and face the court.

Suspectnikoff (*rising*): Oh, okay. I'll stand up, already!

Chairman: Now give us your full name, patronymic and familiar.

Suspectnikoff: Oh, I admit it. I'm Sensky Vladilenovich Suspectnikoff.

Chairman: Who'd you work for before this arrest?

Suspectnikoff: Before this unwarranted arrest, I worked as an engineer at the Scientific Research Institute for Iron-&-Concrete Construction.

Chairman: Your nationality?

Suspectnikoff: Russian.

Chairman: Marital status?

Suspectnikoff: Married. With two children.

Chairman: Have criminal charges been filed against you before?

Suspectnikoff: I've never been arrested before. Or prosecuted. No.

Act I, scene 3

Chairman (*rises, and, with him, the entire performance cast rises*): I declare this court in order. All participants in the hall are advised to remain silent during the proceeding. You must keep completely quiet when the witnesses are testifying. To leave your seats, to cross the hall, or to leave the hall, are categorically forbidden. It's forbidden to talk, to laugh, to pass notes, to make hand-signals, to speak out, or to otherwise respond to the tribunal. It's strictly forbidden to use writing pads, pencils, pens, crayons or chalk, cameras or binoculars, or any other kind of recording instruments. And in the event of the discovery of any technical instruments, they will be immediately confiscated, but the owner will be able to reclaim them when the proceedings are over. Finally, you should notice that this notice is given clearly, so there will be no misunderstandings during the course of this show-trial...

FIRST ACT

*A brief pause, during which **The Secretary** gives **The Chairman** some papers. **The Chairman** removes a pair of spectacles from his pocket and puts them on over the ones he's already wearing.*

Chairman: I will hereby read the court record in the matter of Sensky Vladilenovich Suspectnikoff, married, with two children, non-party member, not previously prosecuted. Suspectnikoff is accused (*looking over the court record, while playing at performing the actions described in the indictment*) of having appeared at a special theater, where a tribunal was in progress. He called upon himself to speak, made certain objectionable remarks about our famous writers and our commercial book trade, stated his preference for subversive literature by foreign bourgeois authors, spouted religious propaganda, spread slanderous disinformation, stating that our criminal proceedings were based upon mere fabrications, and made certain threatening remarks about an imaginary gun, which, allegedly, he was fully prepared to shoot. Additionally, he's been charged with having refused to appear at the court of justice, of refusing to submit to the orders of the chairman of the tribunal, and of having called the allegations of this court absurd, a trashy spectacle, obscenity, rubbish...

Suspectnikoff: What kind of insanity is this!
Chairman: ... insanity...
Suspectnikoff: It's idiotic!
Chairman: ... and idiotic. And as the final result of his refusing to comply with the authority of this tribunal, secret policeman Gorelkin suffered severe injuries and was transported to a hospital, where the doctors fear for his life. All these heinous offenses are substantially premeditated criminal acts, as stipulated in Section 73.A.13(b)(3) of our criminal code, which prohibits disseminating obviously false and pernicious fabrications to accomplish the complete sabotage and subversion of our glorious socialist system, and an insubordinate insult to the authority of the court, by these attempted terrorist acts of...

He falls asleep again.

Chairman: Terrorists... Terrorisimus... Terrrorismism...

He abruptly snaps out of it.

Chairman: Defendant. Do you admit your guilt to these charges?
Suspectnikoff: Of course not! No, I don't.
Prosecutor: Bang, bang, bang! pow! pow!

Chairman: Defendant. As chairman of this tribunal, I need to make clear to you that a frank and complete confession of your heinous crimes and a sincere repentance thereof may, possibly, mitigate your sentence.

Suspectnikoff: But I don't even know what I've done! Let alone what I'm to confess to! And if I did…

Chairman: What's to understand? You really can't say these charges are just fabrication! Now, can you?

Suspectnikoff: That's just it! They're complete fabrications! Outright lies! Or worse…

Prosecutor: Bang, bang, bang. Pow, pow.

Chairman: You really shouldn't talk like that, you know. We've finished, long ago, with the old-style show-trial practice of making fictitious accusations. Now we make nothing but highly realistic accusations, simply to establish your complete and utter guilt of the heinous crimes charged against you. After all, you really can't judge what a pernicious effect you've had on our literary trade, by making those false statements, now can you? You really can't say you didn't talk about the reasons for your existence? Or about god? Now can you? And you really can't say you didn't insult the dignity of this court by showing a childish resistance to its authority? Now can you? Can you? Huh? Now can you? Defendant?

Prosecutor: And besides that… As a result of the defendant's actions, Officer Gorelkin suffered serious injuries, and is now in a critical condition at the policeman's hospital, where the doctors fear for his life.

Chairman: And Gorelkin, I suppose, has children?

Prosecutor: Yes, oh yes. He has many, many children.

Public Defender: Objection, your honor. I know that Gorelkin is childless.

Prosecutor: So much the worse. Maybe he really wants to have children, and now he'll probably die without having the chance to ever have children.

Suspectnikoff: You're making all this up! What am I supposed to have done to him? He's in perfectly good health! And I'm just a little guy. I just popped off some of his buttons, that's all.

Prosecutor: By the way, that was really quite a literary crime. Assaulting an overcoat.[7]

Chairman (*To **The** Prosecutor*): But, what? We can't call this Gorelkin before the court for questioning?

Prosecutor: I think probably we can.

Chairman: But he's suffered some serious injuries.

Prosecutor: Yes, yes, he's really suffered some serious injuries, and the doctors fear for his life. But I guess we'll just have to call him, anyway.

Chairman: We call the witness Gorelkin for cross-examination.
The Voice of Gorelkin: I'm here! I'm here! Already....

Act I, scene 4

Two hospital attendants come on stage with a stretcher, carrying **Gorelkin** with a bandaged head.

> ***Chairman***: Gorelkin, I see you've suffered some serious injuries.
> ***Gorelkin***: Yes, yes. Very serious injuries.
> ***Chairman***: Are you still able to answer some questions?
> ***Gorelkin***: It's difficult for me to speak. With my serious injuries... But I'll do my best.
> ***Chairman***: Just make an attempt to answer, Gorelkin. I've told the section heads about your serious injuries, and I believe they'll richly reward your heroic feat of arresting the defendant, at the proper time.

There's a moment of silence.

> ***Chairman***: Now. Tell us, please, Gorelkin. Are you familiar with the defendant?
> ***Gorelkin*** (*Raising himself up on his elbow, he fastens on* **Suspectnikoff**): I'm perfectly familiar with him.
> ***Chairman***: And what do you wish to say about the facts in this case?
> ***Gorelkin***: Well, then. The facts are like this. Before arriving at the theater as part of my regular duties, I was warned that, during these proceedings, a provocation was likely to be staged by a certain party of subversive foreign elements and other hostile groups. So I was forewarned about what might happen. What Major Korotshev said, was that not only was this provocation highly likely to happen, but it was virtually inevitable, in light of the peculiar character of this theatrical affair. "And it may be necessary," Major Korotshev said, "for you, Gorelkin, and you, Yurchenko, to courageously confront this dangerous provocation, and use whatever means necessary to carry on the struggle against our ideological opponents." Well. So. I, of course, hoped that, in the event that this provocation actually occurred, it would be Yurchenko, and not me, who would have to face our insidious ideological opponents. But still, because I was forewarned, I was prepared for every danger, for every threat. And when I got here, I was told that this dubious person, who was belligerently arguing with his wife, was the guy we were looking for, and

I thought maybe we could just grab him, and he'd submit to identification peaceably. But when we politely requested that he leave the stage quietly, he began spitting out all sorts of cusswords, and flailing and thrashing around, and waving his fists in my face. As a result of which criminal acts, I was given this black eye, here. And also, possibly, severe brain trauma. Or maybe something worse.

Public Defender: But do you really think his actions were premeditated? Or were they merely an act of unpremeditated self-defense?

Gorelkin: Insofar as I was forewarned about this criminal assault, I also thought that his sinister plans were, in fact, premeditated. And criminal, besides.

Prosecutor: That's exactly right!

Chairman: Very good, witness. You may go now.

Gorelkin: Ah, thank you, thank you.

He jumps up from the stretcher and starts to walk away.

Chairman: Witness, where are you going?

Gorelkin: But you said I could go!

Chairman: Yes, I said that. But I didn't mean it literally! I simply meant you were at liberty, in the figurative sense, to step down from the witness stand. But for you to get up and go is, of course, impermissible. Absolutely impermissible.

Prosecutor: Especially since the doctors are still fighting for your life.

Chairman: Lie down, Gorelkin, lie down, now, and our specialists will take care of you.

Gorelkin: Oh, thank you, thank you.

He lies down on the stretcher and they take him away.

Public Defender: Comrade Chairman, it seems to me obvious that the witness is not in a critical condition, if he can just get up off the stretcher and walk away, like that.

Prosecutor: Comrade Chairman, I object. The witness can't just walk away.

Public Defender: But he just now got up and walked away. And we all saw....

Prosecutor: Who says he did that? Huh? Maybe he's just delirious. Or you're just delirious. Or we're all delirious. It happens to me all the time. I know, from personal experience, how somebody gets shot in the head, and all the doctors say, he's about to drop dead. And then he gets up and runs around, like a chicken with its head cut off! Just like that. You see? (*He laughs.*) Like a chicken with its head cut off! Squawking, bawk! bawk! bawk!

Chairman: Please don't remind the court of Gorelkin's injuries. In the Great Patriotic War, on the Eastern Front, of course, everybody suffered injuries, and we still carried on the fight against the foreign enemy.

Prosecutor: And especially the enemies of the People. And, like I always said, at SMERSH, if the little birdies didn't sing for us, and the chickens didn't squawk, we didn't stand for any of this liberal humanist rot. We'd just line 'em up, and bang! bang! bang! pow! pow! They'd all be dead. Like chickens with their heads cut off. Just like it was in the good old days.[8]

Chairman: Oh, all right, all right, already. You don't need to remind the court of those painful things. What happened, happened, and it's over, now, already, right? We just need to get a grip on ourselves and finish this criminal proceeding.

Prosecutor: But why shouldn't we remember the Great Patriotic War? That was our glorious youth! A stunning romantic battle! A roll-call of the spirit! of ideas! of the immortal heart!

Chairman: Proceed, proceed, proceeding. There were many good things, of course, about those good old days. But there were also, admittedly, certain irregularities, in individual cases, in the protocol by which the proceedings proceeded... And now nobody wants to talk about that.

Prosecutor: And now we've put a stop to all that! And now we're spying out anti-socialism, liberalism, humanism, and whoever's not just crazy can just get up on the stage and say whatever they want!

Chairman: And I say, get on with it, already. Do you have questions for the defendant?

Prosecutor: I do. I do do... Do tell us, defendant, how did you break into these proceedings?

Suspectnikoff: What do you mean, break into the proceedings? I didn't break into the proceedings! I just proceeded to come in, like everybody else, through the front door.

Chairman (*quietly*): Defendant, you don't need to speak for everybody else. We're not interested in everybody else. We're just interested in you. And in these proceedings.

Suspectnikoff: And I already told you, I got in here, like everybody else. Through the ticket-counter, with a ticket I paid good money for.
Prosecutor: But who furnished you with a ticket?
Suspectnikoff: No-one furnished me with a ticket. I bought two tickets with my own money. See?
Prosecutor: So where'd you buy the tickets?
Suspectnikoff: From our Party organizer, Comrade **Greenskaya**. She's always got the tickets. And if you don't believe me, you can just ask her.
Prosecutor: We already did. We asked her, already. And when, exactly, did you purchase them?
Suspectnikoff: Two weeks ago. I think.
Prosecutor: Was that the right time to buy tickets?
Suspectnikoff: I don't know what you're getting at.
Chairman: Defendant, be advised. You don't need to know anything. You just need to answer the question.
Prosecutor: And did **Greenskaya** only have tickets for this show-trial? Or for anything else you wanted?
Suspectnikoff: I really don't know. I think she has tickets for various different events. Party events, of course, And for other theaters. For the cinema, sometimes for the "Luzhnik"[9] or for foreign art exhibits.
Prosecutor: But of all these possible events, you chose only this one. Why?
Suspectnikoff: Because when Greenskaya told me that there was a play, called "Tribunal," on the theater bill, I thought it might be something interesting. But if I would have known what a farce this show-trial would be, and how it would turn out for me, would I have come here today? No, of course I wouldn't 've....
Prosecutor: Oh, no! Of course not! And it's not just you! Every criminal who perpetrates a crime tries to figure out how to escape punishment. But if people like you knew that punishment was inescapable for every crime for which there was no acceptable social ground, every crime would be solved, bang! bang! bang! Just like that! And every show-trial would be finished! Pow! pow! Just like that. And then where would we be? (*To **The Chairman**.*) No further questions for this witness, your honor.
Chairman: Does the Defense have questions for the defendant?
Public Defender: I do. I do, too. Tell us, now, Suspectnikoff. Are you sorry about what's happened here?
Suspectnikoff: Sorry! How could I not be sorry! If I'd only known....
Public Defender: No further questions, your honor.

Act I, scene 5

Chairman: We now call the prosecution witness, Lara Suspectnikova, for cross-questioning. Please, Mrs. Suspectnikova. Rise and take the stand.

Larissa: This whole time I've been standing, already. And I've had to just stand here, while you keep insulting my husband.

Chairman: Witness, have you seen what happens to those who refuse to comply with the court's orders? Don't make us make you testify by force. Or rough you up, already. Please rise and take the stand.

Larissa: Oh, okay, I give up. You win. I'll take the stand. (*Rises and takes the stand.*)

Chairman: Witness, the chairman of this court warns you that you must respond to these questions with the truth, the whole truth, and nothing but the truth. If you refuse to answer a question, or if you give a false answer to a question, you may be held criminally responsible for perjury. Is that perfectly clear to you?

Larissa: What's not perfectly clear, already?

Chairman: Please sign the secretary's statement that shows that you've received this warning. (*Larissa signs.*) Now. Witness, are you familiar with the defendant, Sensky Suspectnikoff?

Larissa: How could I not be familiar with him? I'm his wife, aren't I?

Chairman: Witness, you shouldn't comment on the questions. Just answer them as clearly as possible, to the best of your knowledge. For how many years have you known the defendant?

Larissa: For twelve years. I think.

Chairman: And how many years have you been married?

Larissa: Oh, I don't know. I'd have to figure it out. I guess, to start out with, we lived together for three years without getting a marriage license. And then, after that....

Prosecutor: Isn't that illegal?

Larissa (*emotionally*): I told you: Without a marriage license. But because I got pregnant, he proposed, and so we put in an application for a marriage license.

Chairman: Witness, don't quibble about words. Without a license is illegal. And how did that happen?

Larissa: How did what happen?

Prosecutor: He asked you a simple question: How did you happen to enter into this criminal relationship with the defendant?

Larissa: In the usual way. Like everybody else.

Chairman: Witness, don't generalize. Answer specifically.

Public Defender: Comrade Chairman. It seems to me the witness is answering specifically enough. Like everybody else. That means it was love at first sight. A cute meet. The song of a nightingale. Verses of love. Kisses. Poetry, sighs, caresses....

Larissa: How wholesomely you express the whole thing!

Public Defender: Does that mean, that's how it really was?

Larissa: Oh, yes! Exactly like that! But, to tell the truth, as far as love at first sight, cute meets, kisses, sighs, poetry, all of that stuff. There was nothing like that. Caresses, of course, there were. We met at my friend's birthday party. My friend Anna Lubovnaya. We sat next to each other at the table, and he put his hand on my knee.

Public Defender: And you, of course, rebuffed him?

Larissa: Well, yes, I wanted to rebuff him, but then I didn't dare. Because I thought if I rebutted him, the whole thing would just stop. And then where would we be?

Prosecutor: What decadence! What depravity!

Public Defender (*getting interested*): And what next? Please tell the court.

Larissa: And then we talked....

Public Defender (*excitedly*): About poetry? About stars? About nightingales? And all that stuff?

Larissa: Well, no. About something different. He said he had a key. He said his comrade from the office left town and left him his apartment.

Prosecutor: And you agreed to sleep with him, on that very first night?

Larissa: Well, yeah, just like that. Because his comrade from the office was coming back the next night.

Prosecutor: I have no more questions.

Larissa: And then we lived together for three years or so, and he never once, the whole time, even dropped a hint about getting married. And when I got pregnant, he finally made the offer, and we held hands, like children, and walked off into the sunset.

Chairman: That means, you've been legally married for....

Larissa: Nine years, I guess.

Chairman: You have grown-up children

Larissa: Igor's in the first grade, but Sveta goes to kindergarten. She's grown-up, for her age.

Chairman: That means, you've spent the greater part of your whole lives together. And probably nobody knows the defendant as well as you do? Is that right, witness?

Larissa: But of course. I guess.

FIRST ACT

Chairman: And because of this, shall we say, intimacy... The two of you have talked about everything. And the defendant's well known to you, now, wouldn't you say, witness?
Larissa: It's well known to me that the defendant's a good husband, a good father, and, finally, a good man. I know all that very well.
Prosecutor: Bang, bang, bang! pow, pow!
Chairman: Hmmm. A good man. What does that mean, a good man? A good comrade? A good mensch? Maybe, for Eva Braun, Hitler was a good man!
Secretary: Yes, Comrade Chairman, Hitler was a very good man! An extraordinarily good man! And Goebbels was a good family man, too. He poisoned all his children, but he just shot his wife! And then he shot himself!

The whole court laughs.

Chairman: So. There, you see, witness. What happens to good people. But to be a good man isn't always a good character reference. You need to say something more specific about him.
Larissa: I don't know what else to say.
Prosecutor: You could tell us what you know about your husband's hostile opinions toward our great socialist state. You could tell us something like that, you know.
Larissa: I don't know anything about opinions like that.
Prosecutor: Oh, okay, then. So when did you first become familiar with your husband's sinister scheme to break into this show-trial?
Larissa: There you go again! You say we wanted to break in. But we didn't break in, we just walked in the front door. With our paid-for tickets. And when Senya came home from work, we just walked out the door....
Chairman: Comrade Suspectnikova. You shouldn't talk about Senya that way. You should say the defendant.
Larissa: For you, he's the defendant. For me, he's my Senya. And so, like I said, my Senya was walking out, and....
Chairman: Witness, I've already told you. You shouldn't call him Senya, but the defendant.
Larissa: And I already told you, I will not call my husband the defendant! To me he's my Senya. My dearly beloved Senya! Or sometimes Senechka....
Chairman: Witness, I'm warning you to cease and desist....

Suspectnikoff: Lara, I'm begging you. Don't argue with them. You see this whole thing's crazy. And if they arrest you, too, who'll take care of the children?

Larissa: I know, I know, Senya. I really should be more careful. But I just can't call you the defendant. I love you, Senechka....

Chairman (*almost in hysterics*): Witness, what are you doing? I really don't want to punish you. But now you leave me no choice. Guards! Arrest her! this instant....

Suspectnikoff: Comrade Chairman, wait a minute! My wife just didn't think. She's really politically naïve, and she doesn't know what you're saying. This whole thing's all my fault. It's me who just didn't think. When I read the newspapers, I didn't even tell her about it. She wasn't even there. And with her, it's always the same old daily routine. Housework, running around, shopping. And then she has to cook dinner, do the washing, take Sveta to the kindergarten and check Igor's homework, and all that everyday stuff. She doesn't do anything political. (*To Lara.*) Lara, please. don't provoke them. Just call me what they want you to call me. I'm used to it, already. I just love to hear your voice, whatever you say.

Larissa: Senechka! My Senechka!

Prosecutor: Bang! bang! bang! pow! pow!

Larissa (*on second thought*): Oh my defendant! Oh, oh, my dear, dear defendant! (*She starts to sob.*)

Chairman (*deeply moved, sobbing*): I simply must! Oh, I can't resist! Oh, such true, true love! How much she loves him! Yes, she truly loves him! But why does nobody love me like she loves him? (*Weeps.*)

Secretary (*upset*): Comrade Chairman, permit me to object. We all love you. And the People love you, too. Everybody loves you, Comrade Chairman. Everybody, except maybe the defendant.

Chairman: Yes, yes. I know you do. But sometimes, you know, I just wish that it wasn't just The People who loved me, not just everybody all together, but somebody who loved me separately, just for myself, and me alone. Oh, all right, then. We'll continue the interrogation. (*To Larissa.*) You were saying, then, that the defendant was on his way to work, and....

Larissa: ... And he said he'd gotten tickets to the theater. So I said to him, right away, that, of course, it seems silly, but... Well, sometimes I need to get away, to get out among other people, to get away from the housework, the kitchen, the washing, and all those everyday things.

Prosecutor: You mean, you never even tried to talk him out of this crazy scheme?

Larissa: No, I didn't even try. If only I'd known....

Prosecutor (*laughing*): Oh, there you go again! If only I'd known... You should've thought of that before you came to this show-trial! But you know this crime wasn't perpetrated accidentally, on some sudden whim. It was the result, no doubt about it, of some premeditated criminal conviction. You've lived with the defendant for some number of years. Haven't you, more than once, during those boring long years, had the chance to talk with him about his malingering discontent with our glorious socialist system? About his brutal disgust, I might say, his bestial hatred for our great socialist construction?

Larissa: Why are you saying those things? What reason would he have to hate you?

Chairman: What's there to hate? Well, sometimes it happens, a man has, festering and brooding within his soul, when he's lost his job, and his wages are wasting away, when he can't get an apartment, and somebody steps on his feet on the subway, a malingering discontent. The guy gets frustrated, the guy gets teed off. And all those things get to him, finally, and they break him down. Among the People, now, there's always suffering. And, then, at home, too, things start to break down. And in his deepest despair, he blames the government. I hate, he says, this government, this glorious socialist system....

Prosecutor (*picking up the theme*): And he says, Get away from me! I hate all of you! Or maybe he picks up a gun, and the machine gun says, Get them away from me! All these chairmen, all these secretaries, all these prosecutors! Bang! bang! bang! pow! pow!

Larissa: What are you saying now? How can you say that? There's my Senya, right there! He not only never hurt **The Policeman**, **The Secretary** or **The Prosecutor**. He never, in his whole life, even hurt a fly!

Prosecutor: Oh, oh! How hard it is to keep cross-examining her!

Chairman: Never mind that, Comrade Prosecutor. Somebody needs to suffer. And maybe, this time, it's her. Sometimes suffering's hard, but it's necessary for our great socialist system to work. (*To Lara.*) I just hope, for your sake, witness, that you finally figure out, we're not your enemies. We really didn't come to this court to do something bad to you. We just wanted to discuss with you, calmly, what we might do to help you and your husband work things out. But then, you need to help us, too.

Prosecutor: Yes, yes. You do need to help. You do need to talk. Maybe your husband's so sneaky, he hides his criminal opinions even from his wife. But between a husband and a wife, there's such intimacy. He can't help giving away his secretly bestial nature.

Larissa: Ah, ah, now that you mention it. That's a totally different thing. Of course, in certain situations, he sometimes turns into a wild beast.

Prosecutor (*quickly*): And what does he say to you then?

Larissa (*excitedly*): He never says anything. He just snarls and growls.

Prosecutor: And then doesn't his bestial hatred finally expose itself?

Larissa: What are you talking about? What do you mean, hatred? He's expressing his animal passion for me! Only me! He's sometimes impotent, you know. But I remember, another time, when he came home early in the evening. And he was really worn out from work, or from standing in lines all the time. And he had a big bag in one hand and a big bag in the other. And then he just flung the bags out of his hands and threw himself on me, snarling, like a wild beast! And I said, "Senya, what are you doing?"

Chairman: Not Senya. The defendant.

Larissa (*meekly*): Oh, okay, okay! already. I'll say, defendant. But give me time to change my mind.

Chairman: Witness Suspectnikova, you really shouldn't talk like that! You're getting the members of the court all excited. You're having a bad influence on them. And in this sultry atmosphere, it's simply impossible to get to work.

He turns toward the jurors and nods.

Chairman: I declare this court in recess. I need to take something into advisement. This court is adjourned.

Act I, scene 6

*All rise, and **The Chairman**, as if he were unbuttoning the fly of his trousers, but without excessive naturalism, points at **The Statue of Themis** with an obvious intent to bless her with this boyish gesture.*

Secretary (*rushing up to **The Chairman***): Comrade Chairman! Not now, not here!

Chairman (*peevishly*): And why not here?

Secretary: It's just that this isn't a Men's bathroom, but ***The Statue of Themis,*** the Goddess of Justice, you see.

Chairman: Really? I thought that maybe she was Zoya Kosmodemyanskaya.[10] I don't believe in goddesses. And I still think we need to fight against the contagion of religion.

(Striding up to the statue.)

Chairman: And besides, her eyes are blindfolded.

Secretary: Comrade Chairman. She's blindfolded, but the public isn't. And besides that, in your high position, everybody's eyes are upon you.

Chairman: Yeah, yeah. I know. They're watching. It's great to be a popular celebrity, but celebrity has its downside. The public has its curious ways. Okay, so where do I go?

Secretary: This way, please.

The Secretary *takes* ***The Chairman*** *by the hand and shows him through the door, to where* ***The Prosecutor, The Public Defender,*** *and* ***The Jurors*** *are hiding out. On the door is a tablet reading:* ***W.C.*** *Two* ***Security Guards With Submachine Guns*** *are standing outside as an honor guard.*

Chairman: And what's that you've got in your hand?

Secretary *(slightly embarrassed)*: This, Comrade Chairman, is a dictionary of the English language.

Chairman: What?! Why are you studying English? Don't you like your native language?

Secretary: That's just it, Comrade Chairman. I love my native tongue very much. So, for that reason alone, I need to study this language. Because I need to know the enemy, you see.

Chairman: Ah, yes. Well, now, that's, of course, perfectly correct. How many changes have taken place, O Great Wise One, in your education, O Great Father and Teacher of the People! *(Weeps.)* Not for nothing did we suffer, not for nothing did we bite the bullet, suffer from hunger, from cold.... *(Keeps weeping.)*

Larissa jumps onto the stage and approaches the cage.

Larissa: Senya!

Suspectnikoff: Lara!

Larissa: Don't worry, Senechka. I'll fight to set you free! I'll fight until you come home to me!

Suspectnikoff *(fatalistically)*: No, Lara. I don't need to be consoled with these vain hopes. No one ever comes back from this horrible place, alive.

Larissa: Please don't talk like that, Senya. You're not thinking correctly. You need to have hope, you need to believe, you need to keep faith, and, sooner or later, justice will prevail. My father served his sentence in the Gulag, and because he suffered through it, finally, he was rehabilitated.[11] Even though he was already dead. Still, it was a great holiday for the whole family. It'll be the same in your case. I believe that.

Suspectnikoff: You've had enough of those holidays, Lara. Don't indulge in idle hopes. Don't wait for me, Lara. Get married again. You're still young and beautiful, and your salary's not bad, either. You can still find some good man. Only watch out, he doesn't try to drag you off to the theater.

Chairman (*stepping out the door of the toilet, peering discomfortingly about*): What are they talking about? Can this contact between the defendant and witness be permitted? Make them cease and desist at once! Doesn't anybody else want to speak?

The Voice of Gorelkin: I do! I do!

***Gorelkin** appears on stage in hospital scrubs and bedroom slipper, while still flapping the empty sleeves of his bulky military pea-jacket.*

Chairman: Is that you, Gorelkin? Have you gotten all better already?

Gorelkin: Not really, Comrade Chairman. I was on the brink of death and the doctors feared for my life. But when I heard the word that somebody needed arrested, I rushed for the door.

Chairman: Remove the defendant's wife, please, and then take a break. Somebody in your condition needs peace and quiet to recuperate. (*Still hiding behind the door.*) Just make them shut up. Quietly, please.

Gorelkin (*in a stentorian voice*): And now, everybody out! (*Shaking the cage at center stage.*)

Larissa (*standing her ground, stretching out her arms*): Senya!

Suspectnikoff: Forget me, Lara! And don't tell the children I've been arrested.

Larissa: But they'll ask me where you've been.

Suspectnikoff (*being taken away*): Tell them... Say, I got hit by a bus.

Chairman (*Looking out of the restroom, checking out his clothes, signaling with his fingers to the Secretary, whispering to him*): Listen, Comrade Secretary. Is my ass showing?

Secretary: Yes, Comrade Chairman.

Chairman (*astounded*): Yass? Oh, what an ass you are! And where else would we see the You, Ass, Ass, Are? What stupidity! I'm surrounded by asses! (*Slams the door.*)

Act I, scene 7

Secretary (*Walks toward* **Larissa**, *and, opening his phrase book, reads out a few English phrases.*): Al-lo, cum-rad. Ees Mosk-cow a bery, beeg, ceety? Yas, eet ees a bery, beeg, ceety. Mosk-cow ees zee kep-e-tal ov zee Soov-yet Oon-yun. Mosk-cow ees zee een-dust-tree-al cen-tair ov zee Sov-yet Ooo-yun. Der a men-ee fek-tor-ees een Mosk-cow. (*Trying to provoke Larissa.*) Oi, soor-ee!
Larissa: What are you talking about?
Secretary: Oh, is that you? Not thinking of going anywhere, are you? Getting along all right, in there?
Larissa: I'm not just getting along. I'm growing up, already. I'm just trembling with indignation at this injustice you've done. Why have you arrested my husband? What are you doing with him?
Secretary: I, personally, never touched him. That's not my job. I just sit there and write the protocol. Whatever anybody says, I write down. And so if they say, "Shoot him!" I write down: "Shoot him!" And if they say, "Set him free!" I write down: "Set him free!"
Larissa: But you can't really justify your role in brutality and torture, like that. You still participate in all these shameful things.
Secretary: Vell, yes-s. I guess, I part-ee-cee-pate. And you don't? I guess?
Larissa (*amazed*): Me? Oh, yes, of course I participate! But we're playing very different roles, aren't we? Comrade Secretary....
Secretary: Different roles, yes. But the same game.
Larissa: But you have to admit it matters, what role you play in the game. Which side you're on in the plot.
Secretary: Ah, yes, but precisely! You surely must play a part. (*Suddenly leaning toward Larissa.*) In this case, **The Prosecutor**'s dying, and, soon, everything will be different.
Larissa (*Thinking she sees in* **The Secretary** *a secret sympathizer*): Yes? You really think so?
Secretary: I don't think, I know. He's old, sickly, and decrepit. He's always wheezing and coughing. But, in our midst, there are other people. People with modern ideas, who know foreign languages, and who don't like that old school humanism. Our socialist humanism....
Larissa: And you know for sure such people really exist?

Secretary: I don't have the slightest doubt.

Larissa: And you think that **The Prosecutor** will die pretty soon?

Secretary: Oh, I don't know just how soon, but sometime, he'll die, I'm sure. I've never, in my life, seen a single immortal prosecutor. We just need to wait. We need to believe. And we need to hope. Am I right?

*Abruptly noticing **The Prosecutor**'s chambers, changing his demeanor.*

Secretary: Never get stuck on your petty losses, I say. Look around you with clear eyes, and you'll see only the good things in your life. Only build new cities, factories, electrical power-stations....

Larissa: I don't know why you're talking like that.

Secretary: (*going on with his list of achievements*): ... hospitals, sports stadiums, cinema theaters, cultural palaces....

*Rushing up to **The Prosecutor** and parading around with him on the open stage.*

Secretary: Well, say, what's up? Do you think you'll succeed in making your criminal charges stick?

Prosecutor: You'll soon see how they bang! bang! bang! right into place. Everything's perfectly clear.

Larissa: And that's important, too! It's all perfectly clear to me! My Senya's not guilty of anything! He's one of the most innocent people in the whole world!

Prosecutor: Bang, bang, bang! pow, pow! What're you talking about? Nobody's ever not guilty and it's always the same crimes. But if you rough the guilty ones up, kick 'em in the ribs and punch 'em in the jaw, maybe they'll tell you where the corpse is hidden. Maybe they'll help you find the smoking gun. But if they don't confess their guilt and they won't tell you where the corpse is buried, they'll plead "not guilty" on you. They'll try to squirm out of the criminal charges. On the alleged basis of their assumed innocence, which nobody believes in, anyway. Not even them.

Secretary (*eagerly*): I completely agree with you. You express everything so clearly. And, as for me, I'm simply overcome by your excellent rhetorical form. You have such a wholesome, blooming look. I look forward with enormous delight to hearing your indictment speech.

Prosecutor (*cutting off **The Secretary***): Bang! bang! bang! pow! pow!

He rushes off to hide in the wings.

Secretary (*abruptly turning to Larissa*): You see that? Give him a machine gun, and he'll just keep bang! bang! bang!-ing away. Without knowing what he's shooting at.

Larissa: But do you really think he's got good aims?

Secretary: Yeah, not bad, I guess. Some of his good aims get people put into coffins. But he still goes on aiming, and the game goes on gaming, too. And the show-trial goes on. But as time goes on, age and sickness will give him away, and he'll start losing his cases. And then maybe things will change.

He notices ***The Public Defender***.

Secretary: But, of course, we can't just think of our own petty little cases! Just look at what's happening in the big, bad world, out there. The imperialists are trampling on freedom in Lebanon, in El Salvador, and in Nicaragua. In Chile, the fascist police are crushing demonstrations. In England, old people are freezing in their absentee landlord's apartments.[12]

Larissa: What are you saying? What old people? What absentee apartments?

Secretary (*with pathos*): In America, which always preaches about human rights and freedom, ten percent of the workers are out of work. Half the African population suffers from severe malnutrition.

He walks up to ***The Public Defender*** *and starts strolling around with him.*

Secretary: So. Do you think you'll be able to prove the defendant's claims? To get your client off, I mean?

Public Defender: We'll soon see. Everything's not as clear as it seems at first sight.

Secretary: I perfectly agree with you. Everything's more and more not so clear. Between us, though, I'd say you're looking pretty good. I really hope you're in your best form for the rebuttal speeches. I look forward with unspeakable delight to your final defense speech.

Public Defender: I've delivered some winning speeches, in my own time. But I still need to consult with my defense team. That's my sacred obligation.

Secretary: Yes. You have your sacred duty. To defend the dignity of man. And that's a beautiful thing, too!

They all exit.

Act I, scene 8

On the empty stage, a **Stage Worker** *appears. He fixes up the props, walks up to* **The Statue of Themis**, *and switches the hammer and sickle in the scale-pans. From stage right, a disheveled character enters. In his hand, he's got a "Spidola" radio with a crooked antenna.*[13] *Out of the radio comes a shrill whistling, hissing static and other muffled noises. The disheveled character dawdles on stage, picking up and putting down the radio, turning the antenna upside down, and touching it to different objects. He painstakingly checks out various places and positions, trying to see which makes the reception better. Finally* **The Stage Worker** *turns around, comes up behind* **The Guy with the Radio**, *and taps him on the shoulder.*

> **Worker**: Yo, daddy-o! What are you, stupid or crazy? What are you doin' with that thing?
>
> **Guy with the Radio** (*fiddling with the knobs*): Shhh! Hey, listen! Can't ya hear what they're sayin'?
>
> **Worker**: Yeah, I'm listenin', already. And what I hear is: (*Imitates the sounds of sirens.*) Oooo-ooo....
>
> **Guy with the Radio**: Yeah, now you're gettin' it. (*Paying attention.*) Didja hear what they're sayin'? They're sayin' they just arrested some guy at the theater today. Didja see it happen?
>
> **Worker**: Nah, I didn't see nothin'. My job's just to go around during intermissions, seein' what needs fixed up, an' puttin' things in order. An' what happens behind the scenes, I just don't see.
>
> **Guy with the Radio**: How 'dja not see it? A guy got arrested, right there in front o' yer face, an' you say ya didn't see it?
>
> **Worker**: What'd he get arrested fer?
>
> **Guy with the Radio**: It don't say here, what for. He just went to the theater an' they arrested 'im.
>
> **Worker**: Ah, ha! He went to the theater! An' you say they didn't say what they arrested 'im for! Of course he got arrested! Because if ya don't work at the theater, why would ya go there? An', besides that, you, big daddy-o, yer wastin' yer time at the theater, too You must-a had some suspicious ideas in yer head, or ya wouldna come here. An' now you're just rattlin' off about this other guy. Next thing ya know, you'll be dragged in front o' the court. An' then you'll say, I dunno what for....
>
> **Guy with the Radio**: I was just hopin' ya wouldn't fink me off.
>
> **Worker**: I don't give nothin' away, to you or ta them. But in your case (*gestures to the spectators*) I won't answer to them. I won't stick my

neck out for ya. An' if ya go on like that, daddy-o, ya better get outta the way....

The Stage Worker *shoves* ***The Guy with the Radio*** *and tells him to move on.* ***The Guy with the Radio*** *stumbles and falls down. And abruptly from the broken radio comes the sound of sirens howling, mixed with the clear, distinct voice of the radio announcer.*

Radio: As we've already announced, there was an arrest today at the Spetznaz Theater, where a previously unknown nobody, a certain Sensky Suspectnikoff, brazenly and outrageously criticized the injustice of our glorious socialist system and called for the observance of fundamental freedoms and the rights of man, in the Western style... Observers think that the Department of Special Operations, which brought Suspectnikoff to the court and authorized the arrest, was following instructions to get rid of whatever remaining political dissidents and non-conformists still exist in the country, in preparation for....[14]

Guy with the Radio (*hurriedly getting up*): Ya hear that? Now will ya listen to that?

Worker: I di'n't hear nothin' and I don't wanna hear nothin'.

Offstage are heard shrill police whistles.

Worker: Now ya see what ya get for listenin' to that radio-free stuff? Ya hear them callin', now? You, big daddy-o, had better get outta here! Or yer gonna wind up in court....

Guy with the Radio: I'm goin', I'm goin', already. (*Runs away.*)

Worker: An' I didn't do nothin', neither. (*Runs away.*)

Gorelkin appears on stage in pajama bottoms, bedroom slippers, and an official uniform shirt.

Gorelkin (*not finding anybody on stage, addressing the audience*): Which one of youse guys was talking about Suspectnikoff? Huh? Yeah, and who's clammin' up, now? Ya think I don't hear nothin'? Ya think if Gorelkin would just die, he wouldn't hear nothin', anymore, right? Well, yer wrong! See? Cuz' Gorelkin hears all, sees all, knows all! Got that, citizens? (*Whistles.*) Yeah, I'm talkin' to you! Now just stay where ya are. An' Don't leave yer seats! means, Don't leave yer seats! Just show a little discipline. Just show some maturity. Everybody always says, "Don't take away my freedom!" But if ya give 'em freedom, they don' know what to do with it. They just turn everything upside down. So why don't they just give it up? Why, I ask ya? Freedom? Hah! Who needs it? (*He goes on muttering about freedom as he exits.*)

Act I, scene 9

A Prison Guard *with a Kalashnikov, clanking the cage door bolts, opens the door to* ***Suspectnikoff****'s cage and shuts* ***The Public Defender*** *inside.* ***The Public Defender*** *stands in front of* ***Suspectnikoff****, smiling, but with obvious apathy, and without getting a response from the prisoner.*

> **Public Defender** (*sticking out his hand*): Permit me to shake your hand. With all my heart.
> **Suspectnikoff** (*not meeting* **The Public Defender**'*s eyes, sticking out a limp hand*): I wouldn't shake on it.
> **Public Defender** (*shaking* **Suspectnikoff**'*s hand*): Delighted, I'm sure. I'm especially delighted by your courage. By your manliness. By your virility. You spoke your heartfelt convictions so strongly before all those people, I just have to admire you, I admit, Mister Suspectnikoff.
> **Suspectnikoff**: What are you doing, laughing at me? What convictions have I got? I wouldn't die for 'em!
> **Public Defender**: Why are you being so modest? By my thinking, your convictions are perfectly forthright and honest and wholly admirable. And I admire you for them.
> **Suspectnikoff**: Convictions, con-schmictions. All that's just big words to me, not convictions.
> **Public Defender**: Does that mean your convictions aren't sincere? Not completely forthright?
> **Suspectnikoff**: What kind of question is that? You can see for yourself what my convictions have got me! As far as I'm concerned, my high moral character is just so much trash. I'm always sticking my nose in everywhere, wanting to know the what, where, and how of everything. Everything interests me. But you can see for yourself what my curiosity's got me. I'm just wearing prison greens, here, like everybody else. So what are you talking about? What are my convictions? The convictions of a convict!
> **Public Defender**: I'm glad to hear you say that. When a man admits his mistakes and begins to understand the effects of his actions on his family, his friends and loved ones, that's the first step toward correction. And we at the Department of Corrections admire that forthrightness as the first step toward complete and sincere correction. I promise you, if you confess to your recent criminal behavior in The

People's Court with a strong, clear voice, and exhibit remorse, like you're doing now, my job defending you will be a whole lot easier. I might even be able to get you off the hook.

Suspectnikoff (*suspiciously*): I don't know what you're talking about.

Public Defender: Listen. We need to work together on a clear and direct program for your self-defense. Because today, when the court session starts, I'm going to put some words into your mouth. And you, without hesitating, without beating around the bush, without hedging, with all the courage of your manly character, with a quiet, calm, comforting, and profoundly thoughtful voice, are going to say that you've thought about your scandalous behavior, and now you understand how your actions have done so much damage to The People and to our glorious socialist system. You just say you're sorry and....

Suspectnikoff: I don't know anything about that. What damage? What criminal behavior? Oh, yeah, I said some things, but I just didn't think about what I was saying. It just popped out of my mouth.

Public Defender: That's just it! You say you weren't thinking. You didn't understand. And The People's Court will pardon you. Because in the end, **The Chairman** and **The Prosecutor**, they're just people, too. Oh, yeah, they still sometimes act according to the old-fashioned methods, they're old and sickly, too, **The Chairman**'s incontinent, but **The Prosecutor**'s the opposite, he can't go, it's painful, and he gets nervous, sometimes, but, all in all, they're just people. They want to understand and forgive. Of course, they can't just completely acquit you, but, taking into account a frank confession and sincere repentance, they can probably reduce your sentence. They'll probably just give you, oh, five, maybe ten years.

Suspectnikoff (*hitting himself in the head*): Ten years! Ten years!

Public Defender: What are you worried about? Ten years, that's just twice five years. Just two fivers. You'll still be alive, I guess. And just think. Ten years pass by, and your kids are grown up, and you won't have had to raise 'em. And you won't have to vaccinate 'em for whooping cough and diphtheria, either. As a family man, you'll have no more worries.

Suspectnikoff (*burying his face in his hands, through tears*): Ten years! Ten years!

Public Defender: You're just scaring yourself with this little number, ten. But what's this ten, anyway? Nothing but a one and a zero. Just one digit next to nothing. And, besides that, in the course of your confinement, there's always possibilities. The court will take into account your good behavior. And after the first term, maybe you'll get lucky, and get sent to the uranium mines. Those ten years will go by fast, out there in Siberia. And if you work hard enough, after three years or so, you'll be home free.

Suspectnikoff: After three years in Siberia? In the uranium mines? After I'm bald and impotent?

Public Defender: So what if you're bald and impotent? It's a relief, is what it is. You don't need to carry a comb. You don't worry about bad hair days. And you don't have to worry about that other little thing, either. You've already got children, and as for that other little thing, I don't see any big problems, coming your way. Listen, Suspectnikoff, Sensky Vladilenovich, Senya. Just make a straightforward confession and help me out here. And then I'll help you, too. I'll defend you so well, I'll make such speeches for you, you'd never be able to make for yourself. Why, when I'm under pressure, I can come up with such speeches, I'd make Plekhanov roll over in his coffin with sheer jealousy.[15] I'm telling you.

Suspectnikoff: Now you listen to me. Are you, maybe, just a little dizzy? (*Twirls his fingers beside his head.*) Just a smidgen woozy? Or something....

Public Defender (*resentfully*): Are you trying to say I'm crazy?

Suspectnikoff: Yeah, and not only you. **The Chairman**, **The Prosecutor**, **The Jury**....

Public Defender: No, no, Suspectnikoff. That's not right, Senya. You listen to me, Senya. It just can't be, Senya, that the whole world's crazy, but you. Think of it this way, see. Who's in the majority, and who's the minority? Who's speaking for the masses, and who's speaking for himself? Who's standing up for what's right, and who's getting it all wrong? Because if we all think the way that we do, it can't that we're crazy, and not you. Most likely the one who's crazy is the one who's all by himself. The one who's swimming upstream against the great tide of public opinion. The one who's left alone against the great society. The one who's abandoned by his family, his wife, his children....

Suspectnikoff: And you're saying that's me?

Public Defender: Excuse me, Senya. I didn't want to say bad things about you. But if nobody else will....

Suspectnikoff: You know, maybe you're right. Maybe I have gone crazy, sitting in this cage here.

Public Defender: There you go, Senya! Now that's a reasonable assumption! On that grounds, we can make a defense. We'll can call in psychiatric experts and prove you need shock treatment. We'll give you the whole works. You'll be a completely different person and get a completely different sentence. You take your meds, you do your sessions, you get the shock therapy. Then, after five years or so, you'll come out a complete idiot. Nothing will bother you. You'll see everything through those rose-tinted glasses.[16]

Suspectnikoff: No, no! Anything but that! I don't wanna be an idiot! Better I go to prison, better I go to the camps, to the uranium mines, even to the firing squad! But I don't want to be a complete idiot!

Public Defender (*disappointed*): There, now, you see? So who's crazy, now?

Act I, scene 10

The Prosecutor, ***The Jurors***, *and* ***The Chairman***, *walk out arm in arm from the theater wings, followed by* ***The Secretary***. *The sentries rush to their stations and stand on guard.*

Chairman: There, now. That's better. Now we can get on with the case.

Secretary (*as* ***The Chairman*** *breaks away and walks to his seat*): All rise! This court's in session! All be seated. Sit down, already.

Chairman: And now we'll proceed to hear the case of the defendant... The defendant... (*To* ***The Secretary***.) Who are we trying, anyway? (***The Secretary*** *whispers into his listening device.*) Suspectnikoff? Who's that? Oh, yeah. I remember. But what about that policeman? Is he still alive?

Prosecutor: Still alive, I'm told, but the doctors fear for his life.

Chairman: Better he should stick with the doctors. Personally, I got fed up with them. I used to believe in two things: Marxism and medicine. But now, I don't believe in medicine, either. Well, all right, then. We'll get on with the session. We call the witness, Greyana Greensky, for cross-questioning.

Secretary: Witness Greenskaya, Comrade Chairman.

Chairman: Okay, Greenskaya.[17] Where is she, anyway?

Greenskaya: I'm right here, Comrade Chairman.

Chairman: Rise and address the court. (***Greenskaya*** *takes the stand.*) Witness, state your name, familiar and patronymic.

Greenskaya: Greenskaya, Albina Robertsova.

Chairman: Are you familiar with the defendant?

Greenskaya: Yes, we work together at the NEE.[18]

Chairman: What kind of relationship do you have with him?

Greenskaya: We're just colleagues. Co-workers. He's an engineer and I'm an engineer.

Chairman: But as the cultural organizer for the NEE, you did your share of social work?

Greenskaya: Yes, I've done some social work. I also worked for the trade union commission.

Chairman: And you direct a lot of cultural events?

Greenskaya: Yes, obviously. A whole lot of cultural events. We arrange cultural excursions as part of our glorious mission as cultural workers for the Marxist/Leninist Cultural Commission. Why, just last year, we organized a trip to the Golden Arches of Socialism. We took part in the All-Union Rollcall of Soviets, under the slogan, "Nobody Forgets Our Soviet History, In Soviet History Nothing Is Forgotten." We visited "The Great Composer Borodin's Symphonic Panorama." We visited "The Stalinist Museum of Military Strength Through Joy." We visited "The Glorious Exhibit of the People's Economic Achievements." We staged a literary quiz-show with the theme, "The Now and Forever Living Lenin." We had a talk on "The Moral Aspects of the Nutritional Program." We listened to a lecture on "The Communist Task and the Work of the Soviet Writer." We got up two group hikes and combined them with a big mushroom-hunt. And, besides all that, we made collective trips to the cinema, the theater, the court, and so on.

Chairman: And the defendant always took part in these cultural activities?

Greenskaya: Um. Hmm. You know, Comrade Chairman. To be perfectly honest, I don't really know. You know, in certain situations, it's difficult to keep track of people. Some people invent excuses for not joining in. Their mother-in-law's in town, their wife's sick, or their children are crying, or something like that.

Prosecutor: So the defendant always skipped out?

Greenskaya: Yeah, he always skipped out. Especially if the event was a Great Patriotic War Memorial, with a Soviet-based, Marxist/Leninist theme.

Suspectnikoff: Lies! All lies! I participated in the NEE quiz-show on "The Now and Forever Living Lenin," and I contributed a question on Mayakovsky.[19]

Public Defender: Is that right, Comrade Greenskaya?

Greenskaya: Yes, that's right. But Semyon Vladilenovich....

Chairman: Witness, you shouldn't say Semyon Vladilenovich, but the defendant.

Greenskaya: Excuse me, Comrade Chairman. Of course, the defendant is a well-educated man. He knows Mayakovsky by heart, and Ilf and Petrov, too.[20] But when it comes to the Marxist/Leninist political-economic plan, he's mostly apathetic. He's mostly a passive consumer.
Prosecutor: But he came here willingly?
Greenskaya: Yes, he came willingly. I offered him tickets, too, and he was interested in the show. So he asked me what it was about. And I said I didn't know, but I heard it'd be something like a big show-trial.
Prosecutor: And what did he say to that?
Greenskaya: And he said: "Very interesting. I love it," he said, "when somebody gets put on trial!"
Chairman: Somebody else gets put on trial, but not him, huh?
Secretary: Pre-e-e-*cise*-ly! Comrade Chairman. Somebody else, but not him.
Prosecutor: If he's so interested in this show-trial that he bought tickets in advance, maybe we should consider whether he came here with a criminal design, with some hopes of making some profit out of it.
Greenskaya: Yes, I think we should consider that.
Suspectnikoff: Bitch, what are you saying? What profit could I get out of this?
Chairman: Defendant, stay in your cage. And stick to your prescribed speeches. Otherwise, in addition to the crimes already charged against you, I'll indict you for insulting the witness and exerting political pressure on poor little her.
Public Defender: I object, Comrade Chairman. I submit my client's behavior is an unwitting result of the nervous strain he's now suffering. He's not in control of his actions.
Chairman: I know that. It's obvious. That's why, the first time he did it, I just gave him a warning shot. But the next time I may not be so lenient. Are there any more questions for this witness?
Prosecutor: There are. Please tell us, ***Greenskaya***. Were you satisfied by the character of this man who shunned taking part in the soviet social life, and shut himself off in the world of his own selfish, petty interests? Since he worked with you in the collective, did he display the slightest interest your cultural affairs? Did he succeed in making friends with other people in the collective?
Greenskaya: I can't say, exactly. From what I could see, I'd say he made friends with Terrorekin. And during lunch breaks at the factory, they'd play chess together.

Public Defender: Who's this Terrorekin? Is Terrorekin here in the audience?

Greenskaya: Yes, he should be here. I gave him a ticket. I think he's sitting somewhere in the back row now. Do you see him? Anybody?

Chairman (*glancing around*): No, I can't see him. (*Pettishly.*) Give me the binoculars. (**The Secretary**, *immediately, without thinking, brings the binoculars from the exhibits.*) So. Which one is he? Is that him? Crouching down out there? Hiding behind the seat....

Greenskaya: Look, you can see him there, all huddled up, in the back row.

Chairman: The one with the grey pea-jacket. Is that him, comrade?

Greenskaya: Yeah, that's him, I guess. The one in the black-and-white pyjamas.

Chairman: Yes, I see him now. But what's he doing in the back row? Couldn't you have gotten him a better ticket? Like front-row seats, maybe?

Greenskaya: No, no. Our free tickets were all for the best seats. Probably he traded with somebody. He has a certain habit of antisocialism. In meetings, he always wants to sit in the back row.

Chairman: Okay, so just sit there. (*To the audience.*) You, Terrorekin! Get ready! Because we might need you to testify. (*To* **The Prosecutor**.) Do you have any more questions for this witness?

Prosecutor: I do. (*To* **Greenskaya**.) Now tell us, Greenskaya. Did the defendant ever express, in your presence, his brutal disgust with our great socialist system? His bestial hatred of our whole way of life?

Greenskaya: Out loud? In my presence? I never heard anything like that.

Prosecutor: But, if you didn't hear it, and nobody else heard it, doesn't that just testify to his sneakiness, his downright shiftlessness, about his true motivations, which he'd already cleverly disguised?

Greenskaya: I never thought about that....

Prosecutor: That's exactly it. You never thought about it. But now you will think about it. And I'm not afraid to say, if you had thought about it, then, back in your collective days, maybe this whole proceeding might have been avoided.

Greenskaya: Yes, I think you're right. We should have taken into account that it might have become necessary, in the defendant's case, to carry out further cultural educational work.

Prosecutor: And to promote constant vigilance.

Greenskaya: Yes, yes. You're absolutely right.

Suspectnikoff: Nasty, evil woman!
Chairman: Defendant! Wait your turn to speak!
Greenskaya: It's nothing. I'm used to it.
Prosecutor (*with interest*): Has he insulted you like that, before?
Greenskaya: Oh, not like that, exactly. Just sometimes, when he's hungry... (*Getting upset.*) Of course, I don't want to talk about it. But since you already know, I'll tell you the whole story. For the most part, I have to say that Semyon Vladilenovich....
Chairman: Not Semyon Vladilenovich, but the defendant.
Greenskaya: Yes. Excuse me, Comrade Chairman. Of course, the defendant. The defendant mostly displays a shifty, anti-socialist character. He's supercilious and arrogant toward colleagues. He brags about his reading, but he doesn't really know Mayakovsky. Why, sometimes I, for example, read Gorky's "Songs for Stalin's Falcons,"[21] but I don't say I get everything that Gorky says. And I don't brag about it, the way that he does. And, generally, with the colleagues, the defendant's dumbly indifferent. We've sat across from each other, in the factory lunchroom, for ten years, now. And sometimes, you know, I'd wear a different blouse or change my hairstyle. But he never even noticed. He never once said: "Alechka Robertsova, how beautiful you look today. Is that a new blouse you're wearing?" or, "Is that a new hairstyle? Why, Alechka Robertsova...."
Chairman: Not Alechka Robertsova, but the witness.
Greenskaya: But then, Comrade Chairman, if you're going to call me the witness, at least you could ask me, "Where'd you get those stylish shoes? Where'd you get that gorgeous suntan?" Or something like that. But nobody ever pays attention to all those little things. And after all those years, he never even bothered to remember my birthday. (*Sobbing.*) And if he'd thought about getting married, and having a woman around the place, it wouldn't have been the worse for our collective. Or for him, either.
Larissa (*taking the stage*): It wouldn't have been worse for whom? For you, maybe? But Senya always said to me....
Chairman (*menacingly*): Who said what to whom?
Larissa (*To **The Chairman***): The defendant. The defendant said... (*To **Greenskaya**.*) Senya always said to me you were bow-legged and potato-nosed.
Suspectnikoff (*reproachfully*): Lara! Please don't....
Greenskaya (*haughtily*): You don't know what he said to me! He told me once I had a Grecian nose.
Larissa: Yeah, right. Ancient Greek, maybe.

Prosecutor: There. You see how he is. To one woman he says one thing, to another another. (*To **Greenskaya**.*) There, now do you see what a spineless rat you've been sheltering in your collective?

Greenskaya: Yes, of course, I see. Now I see he's the enemy, and maybe deserves to be shot.

Prosecutor (*gleefully*): Bang! bang! bang! pow! pow!

Public Defender: Comrade Chairman, I object. The witness shouldn't give the verdict of the court.

Chairman: That's completely right, Comrade Public Defender. Witness, you need to stick to your assigned script. We can talk about the defendant privately, in chambers, afterwards. But it's your designated role to bear witness to the court, not just gossip about the defendant.

Prosecutor: Comrade Chairman, I don't see why we need to stuff gags in the witness' mouth. Where now is our socialist humanism? After all, she's presenting us with more and more interesting facts about this petty, callous egotist. We're plunging more deeply into his sinister plot, with which he was so obsessed that he didn't even notice how his co-worker dressed herself up for him. And he didn't remember her birthday, either. Even after ten years. And I ask you sincerely: Can even his ostracism from the socialist collective account for his brutal scorn, his bestial repugnance for our whole soviet way of life?

Public Defender: Comrade Chairman, I object. The witness may, of course, express her personal opinions, but she doesn't have the right to dictate how this court's judgment will be carried out.

Prosecutor: Why doesn't she have the right? In our glorious socialist system, every man, or even woman, has the right to judge another man. Or even a woman. And to denounce them. And, after all, she only wants to speak out our whole society's accusations against him.

Chairman: Gentlemen, gentlemen. Please! Proceed, proceed. Proceeding. And if she can prove her accusations, then she can make them. And then her case will be open for questioning, just like everybody else's. Witness, you're free to go.

Greenskaya *steps down into the audience.*

Chairman: We now call witness **Terrorekin** for cross-questioning. Is **Terrorekin** here? (*A pause.*) I'm asking you all out there, where's **Terrorekin**? We're calling all **Terrorekin**s....

Greenskaya (*from the audience*): He was just sitting there, a minute ago.

Secretary: I saw him sitting there, too.
Prosecutor: Bang bang bang! pow! pow! (*Sarcastically.*) I just saw him sitting there! He was just here, a minute ago. That's what they all say. But we don't need to see him, we need to arrest him. It was perfectly clear that he'd run away.
Public Defender: Oh, no it wasn't perfectly clear. It was pretty hard to predict just what he'd do when he was called to testify. Especially since there were people sitting all around him.
Prosecutor: Sure, there were people all around him. But you need to watch out, what kind of people they were. Maybe they all just up and ran out on us, too.

Act I, scene 11

Racket in the wings. **Gorelkin** *enters, dragging* **Terrorekin** *in a headlock.*

Chairman: Now what's this nonsense? What's that you're dragging in?
Gorelkin: What's happening, Comrade Chairman, is that this citizen was trying to run away. So I grabbed him out of a cab.
Chairman: Ah, Gorelkin! Have you recuperated already?
Gorelkin: Nothing like that, Comrade Chairman. I'm still in a lot of pain, and I feel like I'm about to die. But when I saw this guy attempting to make an escape, I just had to grab him.
Chairman (*deeply moved*): You just had to grab him! You were on the brink of death, but when duty called, you bravely responded! We should raise more people like you in our glorious socialist system! (*Weeps.*) Thank you. Gorelkin! Thank you! I believe your brave deeds will be noticed by the head of your section, and our specialists will immediately show their deepest appreciation by giving you whatever care you need to make a complete recovery from your seriously severe, nearly mortal injuries.

The hospital attendants put **Gorelkin** *on a stretcher and exit.*

Chairman (*wiping away tears*): What a guy! A real Hero of the Soviet Union. (*Turning to Terrorekin, reproachfully*) What were you doing, witness? Trying to run away from justice? Aren't you ashamed of yourself?
Terrorekin (*shaking with terror*): Sh-sh-sh-sh-....
Chairman (*imitating him*): Y-yes, y-y-y-you! Your name, familiar and patronymic?

Terrorekin: T-T-T-Terrorekin.
Chairman: T-T-T-Terrorekin? Or just Terrorekin?
Terrorekin: J-just T-T-T-Terrorekin.
Chairman: Familiar and patronymic.
Terrorekin: P-P-P-Peter Sh-Sh-Shinkovich.
Chairman: Peter Shrinkovich?
Terrorekin (*willingly agreeing*): P-P-Peter Sh-Sh-Shrinkovich.
Chairman: What does Shrinkovich mean? Maybe you mean Stretchkovich?
Terrorekin (*agreeing*): N-no, Sh-sh-shrinkovich.
Chairman: Or Stinkovich?
Terrorekin (*agreeing*): St-st-stinkovich.
Chairman (*irritated*): I really don't get you. Do you have your passport with you?
Terrorekin (*agreeing*): Sh-sh-sh-sh....

With trembling hands he turns out his pockets and throws on the floor some papers, notebooks, handkerchiefs, matches, and cigarettes. Finally, he finds his passport and hands it to ***The Chairman***.

Chairman (*reads*): Peter Shiskovich. But you said Shrinkovich.
Terrorekin (*with perfect willingness*): Shrinkovich.
Chairman: Witness, today you'll be cross-examined in the case of Semyon Vladilenovich Suspectnikoff. The court warns you that you must speak the truth, the whole truth and nothing but the truth. And if you refuse to give testimony, or if you give false testimony, you will be held criminally responsible. Now have you been clearly notified of your rights as a witness?
Terrorekin: No-no-no-no....
Chairman: Just sign the papers for ***The Secretary***, saying the warning was given.

Terrorekin *can't make his shaking hand sign the papers.*

Chairman: And why are you shaking like that? Are you cold or something?
Terrorekin: Co-co-co-co....
Chairman: Or maybe hot?
Terrorekin: Ho-ho-ho-ho....
Chairman: Listen. Stop shaking like that. Get a grip on yourself.

Terrorekin *takes the order literally and grabs his sides with clenched hands.*

Chairman: Now, have you calmed down?
Terrorekin: Ca-ca-ca-ca....
Chairman (*imitating Terrorekin*): Ca-ca-ca-ca... You just keep cackling, son, but you can't lay an egg.
Secretary (*clapping his hands and laughing*): Oh, that's a good one, Comrade Chairman! He just keeps on cackling, but he can't lay an egg! What a big chicken he is! Ha ha ha ha ha....
Chairman: And pick up your things. Why are you scattering things all over the stage, like that? What are the pills you've got in those bottles?
Terrorekin (*crawling around on the floor of the stage*): Se-Se-Sed-du....
Chairman: What's that? Seduxin?[22] Just look at him! He's finally calming down....

Terrorekin *holds his meds in his cupped hands and rises to his knees. He gulps down a few pills.*

Chairman: There. Now can you talk?
Terrorekin: Yes, now I can talk.
Chairman: Is it true you're on friendly terms with the defendant?
Terrorekin: Yes, yes, it's true. (*Remembering.*) Or, no, wait. No, it's really not true. We just, like, maybe sometimes... Played chess and drank a few beers....
Prosecutor (*coming back to life*): So you drank a few beers together?
Terrorekin: Why not drink a few beers? Drinking beer isn't illegal yet. Is it?
Chairman: What are you worried about? Of course it's not illegal yet!
Prosecutor: But guys who drink beer together get into conversations. Sometimes intimate conversations... So maybe you might remember what you talked about with the defendant?
Terrorekin: No, I don't remember. Not what about.
Prosecutor: Absolutely not what about?
Terrorekin: Absolutely not what about.
Prosecutor: I just can't believe it. You'd have to be deaf and dumb not to have talked about what you and him no doubt talked about. Let me guess what you talked about. Maybe you talked about... (**Terrorekin** *clams up.*) About women? (**Terrorekin** *keeps quiet.*) About sports? (**Terrorekin** *keeps quiet.*) About politics? (**Terrorekin** *keeps quiet.*) You

mean to tell me you never, ever talked about politics? Not even once? After all those beers.

Terrorekin (*still scared*): Not about politics. Ne-ne-ne-ne-never....

Prosecutor: I just don't believe it! Never once, over a few beers, did the defendant ever mention his bestial hatred for our glorious soviet socialist system? Never once, when roaring drunk, did he ever say that he wanted to get a machine gun and take all the judges and prosecutors and bang bang bang bang bang bang....

Terrorekin (*in horror*): Bang bang bang! Oh my god....

*He falls to his knees, starts wringing his hands, and crawls on his knees to **The Prosecutor**.*

Chairman: Witness, what are you doing?

Terrorekin (*crawling to **The Chairman**, covering his face with his hands*): We really never ta-ta-talked....

***The Chairman** breaks away and jumps back to his chair. **Terrorekin** crawls to **The Prosecutor**, repeating I ca-ca-ca-ca....*

Chairman: Witness, cease these hysterics, this instant! (*To **The Secretary**.*) Calm him down. Immediately!

*The **Secretary** signals to the hospital guards. They stick an enormous syringe through **Terrorekin**'s trousers and carry him limply off on a stretcher.*

Act I, scene 12

Chairman (*after a pause*): Well, I sure hope that we don't have to terrorize him again! Now our specialists can give him the help he so sorely needs, and maybe then everything will be in order. I really don't understand why our cross-questioning gave him a such a nervous breakdown. As far as I can see, there was nothing unreasonable in our questioning.

Prosecutor: Absolutely nothing unreasonable.

Chairman: Although it's my duty, as chairman of this special tribunal, to make sure these things don't happen. Not on my watch. And I want to make clear to you, comrades, that terrorizing the public isn't the purpose of our tribunal. We're not gathered here today to terrorize anybody. And if anyone of us should be called as a key witness....

Prosecutor: Or a defendant, maybe.

Chairman: Don't try to confuse me! If any one of us is called, as a witness or a defendant, we don't need to be worried. Because, as you can see, we never accuse anybody recklessly. We always look carefully into the whole case, and, for that reason, we sometimes raise questions rather keenly. But if the witness answers our questions truthfully and responds to our questions confidentially....

Prosecutor: ...and with loving kindness....

Chairman: ... the witness is never threatened with torture or death. Quite the contrary, we're always glad to help, in every possible way.

*Suddenly an agitated **Spectator** comes rushing onstage. He approaches the edge of the stage and addresses the public.*

Spectator: Comrades!

Chairman: Hey, wait a minute! Who the heck are you?

Spectator: Comrades, I know now that my mouth is gagged. I know now I'm not speaking freely. But I know what's going on here! We came to see a comedy show, to relax and be entertained. But this isn't a comedy show! The devil only knows just what it is!

Chairman: Wait a minute. Who is this guy? Who let him get on stage?

***The Prosecutor**, **The Public Defender**, **The Jurors**, and **The Secretary** shrug their shoulders.*

Spectator: I'm asking you, comrades, what's really going on here? Right in front of our eyes, one of us gets arrested and thrown in a cage, just like a wild beast, and another guy gets terrorized until he loses his mind, and we just sit here gawking and we don't say nothing. Or do nothing.

Prosecutor: This is a provocation! It's an enemy attack! We must immediately respond by going bang! bang! bang! pow! pow! to repulse this scurrilous attack.

Chairman: I ask you, citizen, why have you showed up here? Just who called you here? If you want to appear as a witness, we'll need your full name, patronymic and familiar.

Spectator: Yes, I've witnessed all your criminal actions! I know what's going on here! You're arresting innocent people for doing nothing, and because of nothing.

Chairman: Comrade Secretary, immediately remove this lunatic from the stage!

Spectator: You're the lunatics!

> **Prosecutor**: Comrade Chairman, permit me to speak a few words with this comrade alone. Off the record, of course....
>
> **Chairman**: Yes, yes, go ahead and talk to him. See if you can persuade him to get the help he needs.
>
> **Prosecutor**: Bang bang bang! pow pow! I'll persuade him, all right. I'll persuade him real hard, so I will, Comrade Chairman.

Some strongmen wearing berets grab **The Spectator** *by the neck and drag him offstage.*

> **Spectator** (*ignoring* **The Prosecutor**): Comrades, comrades! Why are you keeping quiet? Now they're arresting me for nothing, and because of nothing, only for speaking out for the love of you!

He disappears into the wings.

> **Chairman** (*sighs*): How hard it is to work with The People! So much disrespectfulness and so much poor breeding! Without looking into the case, without bothering to understand what's really going on here, he jumps up on the stage and disrupts the whole courtly procedure. Now I ask you: What's to be done with people like that?

Act I, scene 13

From the right theater wings crowd noises can be heard.

> **Chairman** (*To* **The Secretary**): What's that noise I hear?
>
> **Secretary** (*Rushes over to the source of the noises and immediately comes back on stage. He grabs* **The Chairman**'s *hearing aid*): Comrade Chairman, representatives of the Soviet Worker's Union have gotten permission to conduct a demonstration in the court's support. And against the defendant, of course.
>
> **Chairman** (*grumpily*): What's this now, a demonstration? What's to demonstrate? And what the heck are they demonstrating against? This is already a demonstration! What do they want to do? Make a big stink about nothing? How sad, that this kind of thing still goes on today in our glorious socialist state. (*To the public.*) But it's a free country, isn't it? And I can't stop you from demonstrating. Can I?

*The **Secretary** signals two **Demonstrators** to come on stage. On their placards is written:*

> **From Evil Roots Come Evil Shoots!**
> **Uproot The Seeds of Evil!**
> **Death to Suspectnikoff!**

*The **Prosecutor** stands applauding. **The Demonstrators**, passing the cage, spit at **Suspectnikoff**.*

> **Chairman** (*deeply moved*): What wonderful people! Dedicated activists, driven by a single purpose! They just couldn't let this show-trial go on without showing their staunch support for the Soviet People's Court! Oh, what a deeply moving display! (*Weeps.*)

Act I, scene 14

*After the demonstration, **Two Guys** show up. They are foreign journalists. One holds a television camera. The other one has an old-fashioned photographer's camera, a tape-recorder, and a stenographer's pad.*

> **Chairman**: Comrades, where are you from? From what organization?
> **Correspondent with Steno Pad**: We're not your comrades! We're for-een djourn-al-eests.
> **Chairman** (*To **The Secretary***): What? What? What did he say?
> **Secretary** (*Speaking into **The Chairman**'s hearing-aid*): He said, they're foreign journalists.
> **Chairman** (*To **The Secretary***): Journalists?!? Journalists?!? Who let these guys in? Who let them get past the door? (*To the Journalists.*) Ah, hello, hello! Welcome to the U.S.S.R., my dear, dear friends! Come on in already! (*He walks away from the bench and shakes the journalists' hands.*) Here, now, allow me to introduce myself and my dearest colleagues.
> *The correspondents shake hands with **The Jurors**, **The Public Defender**, **The Prosecutor**, and **The Secretary**.*
> **Chairman** (*To **The Secretary***): Ask them something in that foreign enemy language, like maybe where they come from, what they want. Something, anything.
> **Secretary**: Eees Mosk-cow a beeg ceet-y?
> **Correspondent**: Oy, zyour Een-glees ees soy goodt. Where'd you study English? At the Soviet Language Institute in Stalinabad?
> **Secretary**: Yees, Mosk-cow ees a bery beeg ceet-y!

Correspondents (*slightly irritated*): You listen up, bud. We pretty well know that Moscow's a very big city. But what we really want to know about is the show-trial of the Soviet dissident, Sensky Suspectnikoff.[23]

Chairman: What? What? What did he say?

Secretary: He said something about the dissident, Sensky Suspectnikoff.

Chairman: Dissident Suspectnikoff? Dissident, schmissident! What's going on here? Another provocation!?! Another demonstration!?!

Suspectnikoff (*from the cage*): Your dishonor, I object! I'm not a dissident! I'm just a regular guy.[24]

Chairman: There now. You see? He's just a regular guy. Why are you insulting him with all these funny foreign names?

Prosecutor: Bang bang bang! pow, pow! It's that socialist humanism again, Comrade Chairman. Maybe you should bash him in the head with that camera of his.

Correspondent: What'd that guy say?

Chairman: **The Prosecutor** told you that there's no Soviet dissidents here. This is just a show-trial, a performance, a spectacle. Get it? Performance artists. A spectacle. A show-trial.

Correspondent: I know that it's just a show trial. But if it's just a show-trial, what role is that gentleman playing in the cage there? The role of some wild beast, maybe?

Suspectnikoff: I'm playing the role of an idiot.

Secretary: Zyou zee? Kee ees play-eengk zee role ov een eed-jot!

Larissa (*jumping on stage*): No he's not! I don't agree! That's a slander! A libel! A smear! Citizen correspondents! My husband's an innocent man! He was arrested for nothing! And because of nothing! He was arrested for making fun of all the stupid, idiotic things they say in this stupid show-trial! Like, for example, they say he shot Chekov with a submachine gun.

Correspondent: And do you swear that he didn't shoot Chekov with a submachine gun?

Larissa: Oh, of course not! No. Chekov's one of our writers, a classic Russian writer! He died at least a hundred years ago!

The Correspondents write something in their steno pads.

Larissa: Go ahead, write, write! But when you do, write this: They say that he shot Chekov, who's been dead a long time ago. That's what got him arrested. That's what he's on trial for. But it's a big lie. So when you write about Suspectnikoff in your foreign newspapers, and show him on TV, just say he's not guilty of anything. He's a good, simple man, a good-hearted engineer, a good family-man, a beautiful husband and father, with a wife and two children, too. Listen. I'm pleading with you. You don't have to fight to speak the truth, over there, like we do here. Call some meetings, call some demonstrations, march around with placards and slogans, like: **Hands off Suspectnikoff! Free Suspectnikoff! Justice for Suspectnikoff!** Or whatever you like. But, whatever you do, please help set my husband free.

Prosecutor: Bang! bang! bang! pow! pow!

Chairman: Witness Suspectnikova, please think about what you're saying.

Correspondent: Does that mean you don't agree that Suspectnikoff is a big idiot?

Larissa: How can you say things like that? You can see him there now, right in front of your faces. You can see how clear and noble the bright light in his eyes really is. How can you call him an idiot? It's me who's an idiot! Because I didn't talk him out of going to this trashy performance. This stupid show-trial.

Correspondent: I didn't get all that. Does that mean he's not an idiot, you're an idiot?

Secretary: Dere ahr men-ee ee-dee-yots een Mosk-cow.

Prosecutor (*jumping on stage, rushing up to the correspondents*): Now, proceed, proceeding! Comrade foreign correspondents! We'll take no more questions from the likes of you! Who's an idiot, who's not an idiot, that's not for you to decide. We have enough idiots here, without you getting involved. Take a good look around you, and all you'll see is idiots!

The Prosecutor *pushes the foreign correspondents and they stumble offstage, while* **Suspectnikoff** *and* **Larissa** *and the members of the court are left on stage.*

Act I, scene 15

Chairman: Well, now! Finally! We're left with just us. Now maybe we can get on with our work. (*He rises and together with him all members of the court arise.*) The court will proceed to hear the rebuttal speeches. **The Prosecutor** will give his speech for the prosecution. (*All are seated.*) Proceed, proceeding, please.

Prosecutor (*Rises and walks on stage. He speaks sluggishly at first and becomes more and more animated as he goes along.*): Comrades of the court! We live in prodigious times, when all our people work together in a single inspired outburst to execute and fulfill, even to exceed, yes, over-exceed, our allotted quotas, making our lives better, and even more beautiful. But our big happy family, our glorious socialist system, is not without its freaks and misfits, and one of those freaks and misfits sits here before you today. His despicable criminal acts are objectively set forth in the evidence before you, and I won't dwell upon them further before you now. I'm troubled by something else. I'm tormented and tortured because I simply can't understand how our glorious socialist system can nurture such a deeply rooted criminal nature. How, I ask you, in our big happy family, in our tranquil workplaces, in this very court, did he unnaturally conceive his far-fetched, soulless, and, I'd even say, his sinister, evil schemes? Oh, I know, I know, you object, you say to me, he never expressed his convictions openly, he cleverly concealed his brutish, bestial nature. Yet somehow, this great deception eluded all of us here. And I put the question to you: Why did none of our big happy family, why did none of his colleagues at work, why did none of his neighbors in this audience, why did none of us think to fear him, to raise the strident alarm of our glorious socialist society and alert our competent organs, the security police, to his clearly present danger? And now I'll tell you why! Because everywhere a Suspectnikoff works, unknowing and unknown, there secretly festers and breeds an unhealthy atmosphere of permissiveness and leniency, of daydreaming and muddle-headedness. Yes, every day of the week, Suspectnikoff went to work in the ironwork-&-concrete factory, he drew up his blueprints, he drank a few beer, he played chess with his buddies, and then he went home and watched TV with his wife and family. And he thought to himself, without anybody knowing: If only I had a gun, I'd shoot all these TV announcers, I'd shoot all these hockey-players, I'd shoot these performance artists at their show-trial.

Suspectnikoff: Lies! Lies! All lies! I never thought anything like that.

Prosecutor: There, now, you see? He's remorseless! He stubbornly persists in defending himself, he changes colors like a chameleon! Comrades of the court, our glorious socialist system has many enemies. But these enemies are deceptive. There are enemies, right here now, among this audience, whom we can't even see. They walk right up on stage, and blatantly, I say to you now, they baldly display their bestial hatred for our whole way of life. The fight against these enemies isn't difficult, it's not complicated. You simply take them, line them up, and bang! bang! bang! pow! pow! They're all taken care of. But a much greater danger to our glorious socialist system is presented by the Secret Suspectnikoffs among us. Because they are legion. Why, right now, in this very hall, in this audience, there are a thousand secret enemies, who go to work, drink beer, play chess, and cleverly hide their bestial hatred for our glorious socialist system so thoroughly and skillfully they won't be detected by our secret policemen. To describe this sinister thing lurking secretly among us, I coin a word, which you may've heard spoken here among us today. I call it Suspectnikoff-ism! Here let the word ring out! Suspectnikoff-ism! is what I call it. And so it is....

Cries from the Audience: That's right! It's Suspectnikoff-ism! And they're Secret Suspectnikoffs!

Prosecutor: And I regret to say, the sickness called Suspectnikoff-ism has spread its sinister disease in our glorious socialist system. This Secret Suspectnikoff-ism has infected all the cells of our society, like a virulent bacillus. It organizes conspiracies, it stands at the machines, and it sits in meetings, at conferences and in tribunals. (*Suddenly explodes.*) Yes, look around yourself now! And look at yourself! Take a good look at the audience! Get a good look at these people! And then you'll see why I say: They're all Secret Suspectnikoffs, too! And I ask you, citizens: What can be said in defense of this audience? Comrades of the court! If you take a good look at yourself, and take a good look at your neighbor, and don't just sit there gawking, you've really got to see, that whoever's sitting next to you is just a Secret Suspectnikoff, too!

Cries from the Audience: That's right! He's absolutely right! They're all Secret Suspectnikoffs!

Prosecutor (*fervently prompting the crowd from the edge of the stage*): Wait, now. Who said that? What do you mean when you say, "That's right?" (*To the crowd.*) There now, you see! Don't you? It's a Secret Suspectnikoff who cries out, "That's right!" To disguise his own bestial nature. And we're just wallowing in scum and garbage, wrecking the bad comedy, going on and on about our socialist humanism! Until that socialist humanism finally picks up a submachine gun and points it at all of us....

He takes the Kalashnikov out of the hand of **The Statue of Themis**.

Prosecutor: And says: Bang! bang! bang! pow! pow! Now you're all dead!

The Prosecutor *cocks the bolt, intending, apparently, to start firing at the audience.* **The Secretary** *throws himself on* **The Prosecutor**'s *back. Secret Policeman* **Gorelkin** *comes to* **The Secretary**'s *defense. Noises, hubbub and uproar, cries: "Ow!" "He's out of* *his mind!" "Grab the gun!" etc. Sharp bursts of submachine-gun fire come from somewhere offstage. Now every member of the court throws himself on* **The Prosecutor**.

The Voice of the Chairman: Somebody call the police!

The stage-lights are extinguished. The sound of sirens is heard coming closer. The stage is lit up again by flashing lights, showing **The Prosecutor** *laid out on a stretcher and taken away. The lights are extinguished and then flare up again. The court members stand at their stations.*

Chairman (*impassively*): This court stands in recess.

Notes

1   "The Bard" is a stereotyped figure of the 1960s Soviet dissident period. As Irina H. Corten notes:

> Known in Russia since the eighteenth century in its original English meaning [...] this word ["bard"] acquired a new connotation in the late 1950s and 1960s. During the cultural "thaw" [...] which followed Stalin's death, non-conformist poet-singers, or bards, began to give informal recitals with an anti-establishment slant. Some of them, such as Alexander Galich, were well-known dissidents. The two most famous bards of the 1960s and 1970s were Burlat Okudzhava and Vladimir Vyotski.

Vocabulary of Soviet Society and Culture (Durham: Duke University Press, 1992), 21. These Soviet bards might also be compared to the East German dissident, Wolf Biermann, and the American folk singer, Bob Dylan.

2   Anton Pavlovich Chekhov (1860–1904), perhaps the most famous Russian playwright, was also an author of short stories. In the international context, he was an influential figure in the rise of modernism.

3   Voinovich is here clearly criticizing the atmosphere of political censorship of Russian writers and foreign literature under the Brezhnev regime. As Rosalind J. Marsh observes:

> Firmly established in power by the end of the 1960s, the Brezhnev administration imposed more effective, less unpredictable controls on literature than Khrushchev. [....] The Soviet leadership continued the policy which Khrushchev was pursuing [...:] the encouragement of the publication of mediocre, ideologically correct writing for the masses, an attempt to prevent the circulation of works which might be construed as actively anti-Soviet, and the desire to pacify the liberal intelligentsia by permitting the small-scale publication of some excellent books and articles. [...]. The publication of such interesting works [as Proust, Joyce, and Kafka] in small editions [...] led to a situation in which, as Klaus Mehnert observes, there are "too many Russians chasing too few books".

Soviet Fiction since Stalin (London: Croom Helm, 1986), 16. Ironically, however, the official censorship of Russian literature under Brezhnev resulted in a flourishing of unofficial literature. "Both *samizdat* and *tamizdat* reached their apex under Brezhnev, involving such authors as Solzhenitsyn, Josif Brodsky, Vladimir Voinovich, Georgi Vladimov and Venedikt Profeev. A beneficial side-effect of *samizdat* was, as Andrei Sinyavski observed, that some of the official publishable authors were compelled to write more daringly, 'for the sake of their own self-respect.'" Herman Ermolaev, *Censorship in Soviet Literature, 1917–1991* (Lanham, MD: Rowan and Littlefield, 1997), 144–45.

4   The aphorism, "Where there's a man, there's a problem. No man, no problem," is attributed to Stalin in Anatoly Rybakov's novel, *The Children of the Arbat* (1987). But in *The Novel of Memories*, Rybakov later admitted he wasn't sure of the source for this statement. "It's possible I heard it from someone, it's possible I made it up." wikiquote.en/wiki/Joseph_Stalin_and_magazines.russ.ru/znamia/1998/1/lipkin.html.

5   Voinovich satirizes "Soviet humanism" in "A Fourth Aspect of Humanism": "Advocates of so-called socialist humanism always thought that, unlike ordinary humanism, theirs was inseparable from cruelty and hatred—in the name of a higher end, of course." *The Anti-Soviet Soviet Union*, trans. Richard Lourie (San Diego: Harcourt Brace Jovanovich, 1985), 284.

6   The strip-search performed on Suspectnikoff is a black humor version of the notorious procedures performed on political prisoners by the KGB in the Lybyanka prison, as described in numerous works of Soviet dissident literature. The object of these searches was to humiliate the prisoner and break down his resistance to making a confession under coercive interrogation and torture. A typical feature of these searches was to strip off the detainee's belt and pop the buttons off his trousers, forcing him to constantly try to hold up his pants and not dirty himself while still undergoing interrogation. See, for example, Vasily Grossman, *Life and Fate*, trans. Robert Chandler (New York: Harper and Row, 1985), 615–37. Nadezhda Mandelstam, *Hope against Hope*, trans. Max Hayward (New York: Athenaeum, 1970), 74–88.

7   A reference to Nikolai Gogol's famous short story, "The Overcoat" (1842). Voinovich's *The Fur Hat* can also be considered a satire of Gogol's story, and Voinovich has often been called "a latter-day Gogol."

8   SMERSH (*smert' shpionem*; literally, "Death to Spies") was a "security organ created during the Second World War for tracking down and liquidating any elements within the U.S.S.R. considered to be a threat to the country's security." Barry Crowe, *Concise Dictionary of Soviet Terminology, Institutions, and Abbreviations* (New York: Pergamon Press, 1969), 135.

9   The "Luzhnik" is an Olympic Sports Stadium in Moscow. It was built in 1955–56 and originally named the "Central Lenin Stadium" or "National Stadium of Russia." It was the main arena for the 1980 Summer Olympics. Voinovich's satiric reference here perhaps has to do with the fact that the Soviet authorities unsuccessfully attempted to expel him from Russia before the 1980 Olympics.

10 Zoya Anatolyevna Kosmdemyanskaya was a Soviet partisan who was captured by the Germans while carrying out acts of sabotage and executed on November 27, 1941. When Stalin read her story in *Pravda* in 1942, he exclaimed: "Here's the People's heroine!" and Kosmodemyanksya was celebrated as a Hero of the Soviet Union. See https://en.wikipedia.org/wiki/Zoya_Kosmodemyanskaya.

11 As Alexander Solzhenitsyn observes in *The Gulag Archipelago*, the Soviet authorities often made promises of amnesties to be declared for Gulag prisoners and Soviet exiles, some of which were actually fulfilled. Most were not. Even if a prisoner were released from the Gulag, he might still be kept in exile in Central Asia. See Solzhenitsyn's accounts of Stalin's World War II victory amnesty in *The Gulag Archipelago*, 1918–56, III–IV, trans. Thomas P. Whitney (New York: Harper and Row, 1975), 187–91; and of "the 'Voroshilov amnesty'" in *The Gulag Archipelago*, V–VII, trans. Harry Willetts (New York: Harper and Row, 1978), 437–39.

12 These denunciations of "the West," and especially the United States, for its imperialist ambitions and civil and human rights violations, whether valid or not, were a standard feature of the political rhetoric of the Soviet authorities during the Cold War era and were also repeated by Western leftists.

13 A *Spidola* radio "was the first mass produced transistor radio with short wave based in the Soviet Union. […] In some cases, the Spidola was used to listen to the *Voice of America*. The processing of at least one Soviet dissident involved confiscation of the Spidola as an 'instrument of crime.'" http://en.wikipedia.org/wiki/VHF_Spidola. In Soviet jargon, *radiovoina* ("radio war") and *televoina* ("television war") were "terms […] used in official parlance during the Khrushchev and Brezhnev eras in reference to anti-Soviet propaganda that presumably was waged by Western broadcasting companies" or by semi-official government agencies like Radio Free Europe's Radio Liberty. "Unofficially, however, the terms were used in the opposite sense, in regard to anti-Western propaganda on Soviet radio and television." Corten, *Vocabulary of Soviet Society and Culture*, 120. See also n. 7 supra.

14 During testimony regarding implementation of the Helsinki Accords to the US Congress, Rep. Patricia Schroeder (-CO) testified that "the Soviet government has apparently taken upon itself to use the [1980] Olympic games [in Moscow] as an instrument and an opportunity to punish and deter dissidents within its own country." *Hearing before the Commission on Security and Cooperation in Europe*, June 6, 1978) (US Government Printing Office, 1978), 38. Protests were also made regarding Vladimir Putin's use of the 2014 Winter Olympics in Sochi for propaganda purposes, especially after the 2008 Russian attack on Georgia.

15 Georgi Plekhanov (1856–1918), sometimes called "The Father of Russian Marxism," was a Russian revolutionary and Marxist theorist who later clashed with Vladimir Lenin over the direction of the October 1917 Revolution. Despite his opposition to the Bolsheviks, Plekhanov was still idolized by the Soviet Communist Party as a founding father of Russian Marxism. In earlier years, Plekhanov delivered a speech at a rally at Kazan Cathedral demanding the release of Nikolai Chernyshevsky (the imprisoned author of *What's to Be Done?*) that galvanized the masses and sparked a popular revolt. See John and Carol Garrand, *Inside the Soviet Writer's Union* (New York: Free Press, 1990), 19–20.

16 The psychiatric incarceration of Soviet political dissidents, under the official rationale that anyone who questioned the essential sanity and rightness of life in the Soviet Union and of the Communist Party leaders was, ipso facto, insane and was a notorious feature of Soviet policy. In Soviet slang, the terms *durdom* (from *durak*, "fool," and *dom*, "house") and *psikhushka* (from *psiki*, "psycho") were "often used specifically in reference to the Soviet government's practice […] of punishing dissidents by placing them in insane asylums." Corten, *Vocabulary of Soviet Society and Culture*, 44, 119. The purpose

of this psychiatric incarceration was to break the dissident's resistance and force him to conform to official policy.

17 The name *Zelenya* ("Greenskaya") is obviously allegorical, although its precise reference is obscure. In Voinovich's *Tribunal, Zelenya* is a Communist Party activist and Soviet cultural organizer who works to drum up popular support for cultural events and to ensure conformity to cultural policies. Her work is similar to that of the *zelenyii patrulii* or "Green patrols," which were "voluntary citizens organization[s] devoted to maintaining the health of trees and other vegetation in urban areas. In the Brezhnev era, this was one of the few public organizations whose members served with genuine dedication and enthusiasm." Corten, *Vocabulary of Soviet Society and Culture*, 160. But *zelenen'kie* ("little green ones") was a Soviet slang expression for American dollars. In the Russian Civil War, the "Greens" were an independent army that opposed both the "Whites" (the czarists) and the "Reds" (the Bolsheviks or Communists).

18 The term "NEE" (*Naychno-Issledobatel'skii Instityt*) or "Scientific Research Institute" was "a very common component of abbreviated terms" for official entities in Soviet jargon. See Crowe, *Concise Dictionary of Soviet Terminology*, 95.

19 The Russian Futurist poet, Vladimir Mayakovsky (1893–1930), was an early believer in the 1917 Bolshevik Revolution and a supporter of the Communist Party during the Russian Civil War of 1917 to 1922, who allegedly killed himself on April 14, 1930, when his early dreams of a utopian socialist society were betrayed by the Stalinist terror, and a passionate love affair with the Russian actress, Veronika Polonskaya, went bust. Persistent rumors, however, suggested he was killed by the KGB.

20 Ilya Ilf and Yevgenii Petrov ("Ilf and Petrov") were Soviet fiction writers who collaborated on two wildly popular satiric novels, *The Twelve Chairs* (1928) and *The Little Golden Calf* (1931), that showed Soviet society from the outsider's perspective of their main character, a Russian con-man, Ostap Bender.

21 During World War II, the Soviet air force was colloquially referred to as "Stalin's falcons," an allusion to Maxim Gorky's story, "Songs of a Falcon."

22 In Voinovich's account of his troubles with the Soviet authorities following his protests of the Sinyavski/Daniel trial, he observes that the constant persecution and harassment drove him into "consuming several packets of Seduxin and Tyleval." *The Ivankiad*, trans. David Lapega (New York: Farrar Straus & Giroux, 1976), vii.

23 The Soviet dissident movement, like Voinovich's political activities,

> began after the government crackdown on the creative intelligentsia, initiated at the political trial of the writers Sinyavski and Daniel in 1966. [...] The dissident movement expanded and grew rapidly in the late 1960s and reached its apogee in the early 1970s; the writings and activities of Alexander Solzhenitsyn [and of Vladimir Voinovich!] played a significant role in this process. Solzhenitsyn's forced departure from the USSR in 1974, as well as the imprisonment, psychiatric confinement (see *durdom, psikhushka* [and note 13 above]) or exile of other dissidents gradually decimated their ranks. The dissidents of the 1960s and 1970s did not present a united ideological front. [...] What they had in common was the belief in the importance of human rights and freedom of expression.

Corten, *Vocabulary of Soviet Society and Culture*, 56.

24 Cp. Voinovich's statement:

> I've often said that I do not consider myself a dissident, although by all the formal indicators I was. I wouldn't say I acted to defend human rights as a whole since I limited myself to defending the rights of just a few individuals. Besides that, I was published abroad. Moreover, whenever they threatened me, I would take up the challenge, and that was always a source of some pleasure. In fact it was the authorities themselves who were to blame. I believe a citizen has a duty to be loyal, but the state has a duty to be loyal to the citizen. I'm not for smashing the state. Everybody knows what would come of that. The collapse of the government would be a terrible tragedy for millions of people. For that reason I do not consider myself a dissident in the political sense.

Vladimir Voinovich, *Conversations in Exile: Russian Writers Abroad*, ed. John Glad (Durham: Duke University Press, 1993), 93.

FIRST INTERMISSION

SECOND ACT

Act II, scene 1

The Bard *walks on stage, and, after tuning his guitar, he quietly sings:*

—Why do flowers grow?—
A child wanted to know.
The little flower answered:
—Only flowers know!
—But is there any use for flowers
If they just blossom and blow?
—Of course there is!
The little flower answered.
—Because if flowers didn't grow
The earth would just wither and blow
Without leaving a flower or a leaf.
Everything on earth is brief.
But before the flower grows
     And withers and blows
It must become the full-blown rose.

After a brief pause, ***Larissa*** *shows up with a shopping bag.*

    Larissa (*out of breath*): Excuse me for interrupting. What, is everything over, already?
    Bard: What do you mean, is everything over? What did you have in mind?

Larissa: I just want to know what's happened to the court. You know, the show-trial.

Bard: Ah, the court! The show-trial! They're still in recess. They haven't started the proceedings yet. And maybe they won't get started anytime soon, either. Something's happened to **The Prosecutor**. Maybe he's gone crazy, maybe he's had a nervous breakdown. Nobody knows for sure. Some people say he's dead.

Larissa (*clapping her hands*): Oh, what good luck!

Bard: Yes, but that's just rumors. Nothing's certain about this case. The authorities are keeping the whole thing hushed up. They don't want to admit that **The Prosecutor**'s death has put a stop to the show-trial. They don't want to admit that the show-trial won't go on.

Larissa: Oh, I'm still so glad! Because **The Prosecutor** really was an evil, evil person.

Bard: **The Prosecutor**? An evil person? Well, yes and no. He was an Old Bolshevik, you know. But maybe he wasn't just evil. Maybe he was just old-fashioned. Maybe he was just what they call an Old School person, who didn't know how to change, and couldn't be any different than he was.

Larissa: And what about **The Chairman**? Is **The Chairman** an Old School person, too?

Bard: Yes, of course, **The Chairman**'s an Old School person, too. But, you know, those Old-School People really aren't all bad. There are all kinds of Old School People. Grandmothers, fishermen, drunks....

Larissa: And **The Jurors**? What about them? Are they Old School People, too?

Bard: You know, after thinking about it, I finally came to the conclusion there's something good in all people. Even Old School People. And if you look at **The Secretary**, now, he's really a completely modern man. And he's very well-educated. He knows Tyutchev[1] by heart, he wears jeans at home, and he listens to jazz. And, like you've maybe heard, he even speaks English in court.[2]

Larissa: How nice you make it all sound! You give me hope that maybe someday the New School People will bring a breath of fresh air to the old socialist system. Do you think they might pardon him?

Bard: What? Who? Pardon him?

Larissa: I'm thinking of my husband.

Bard: Pardon your husband? No, I really don't think so. The whole system's been set in motion. The proceedings are already proceeding. And you know what they say: The show-trial must go on. And where there's a show-trial, they need somebody to try. What would the Old

School People do, if they didn't put your husband on trial? The whole system would break down, if they didn't have somebody to try.

Larissa: But you just said they're all good people!

Bard: Sure, they're all good people. But they have families to think of. They need to feed and clothe their children, set them on their own two feet, and make them into Old-School People, just like them. (*Sings.*) "Because if flowers didn't grow, their lives would just wither and blow...."

Larissa (*interrupting* **The Bard**): Yes, but, excuse me, please. I want to ask you something. If there's no public defenders to help my husband here, in the Soviet Union, maybe I could appeal to some foreign lawyers. I've heard that, in the West, there's a big outcry, now, about human rights. They say there's some kind of citizen's association for my husband's defense, called *The Committee in Solidarity with Suspectnikoff*.

Bard: Well, now. What about that? That's not bad for you. And if there weren't rumors, there wouldn't be a public outcry, now would there? They're interested in your husband's defense as a Soviet dissident in this mock-up version of the Moscow show-trials. Because without him to defend, they wouldn't have anything to do with human rights. (*Sings.*) "Because if they didn't grow, their lives would just wither and blow...."

Larissa: But I want you to defend my Senya!

Bard: Do you really believe in him?

Larissa: Can you really doubt it?

Bard: I don't know. I really don't. It just seems to me that your position has changed for the better. You're counted among the important people now. Before, you were just the wife of some unknown engineer. A housewife. A nobody. Now, you're the wife of a famous Soviet dissident. And the Committee knows your names. His name and yours. So they're interested in you, too. And that's good news for you.

Larissa (*passionately*): Do you really believe I need a *Committee in Solidarity with Suspectnikoff* to take care of poor little old me? I don't need a committee for me! I need a committee for my husband! I need my husband and my children need a father! We're his family! We love him! And we love him just the way he is: clumsy, abused, unimportant. We'll still defend him! And you can defend him, too! And then you won't have to admit what a cynic you really are. You keep on pretending that you're not embarrassed to admit what you really are: a bard and not a fighter. But I'm not ashamed of fighting. I'm ashamed of making up excuses not to go on fighting. And I'm going fight for my husband.[3] Whatever way I can....

She sees **The First Juror** *come on stage and follows him.*

Act II, scene 2

The First Juror *comes on stage, partly arguing with himself, partly addressing the public.*

> **Juror**: And, ir-regardless of what I see happening, right in front of my face, considering the whole thing objectively, I'm really an optimist. I believe that slowly, gradually, the whole world's getting to be a better place. Every day, every way, things are getting better. It's just that some stupid people can't see these trivial events in the bigger world-historical perspective, like I can. Take this case, for example. This petty show-trial. There's such a big public outcry and so much static and noise about this trivial case. About this Suspectnikoff. But if you look at him standing there, right in front of your face, you'll see, it's all just noise about nothing. What's this Suspectnikoff, anyway? A Soviet dissident? Like the Western press says? Or an enemy of the People? Like they say over here... It used to be it happened during the cold dark night, and nobody saw what happened. They took them by the dozens, without bothering with witnesses. But now they single out just one unlucky suspect and put him through this big show-trial. And still the people just sit there, looking around and blinking, seeing nothing, saying nothing, like nothing's happening. And if you don't protest, pretty soon it's all over. There's no man, and there's no problem. You might as well just sit and wait until the whole thing's over, maybe pick up a snack at the snack bar, or something.[4]
>
> **Larissa** (*She stands by, waiting, until* ***The Juror*** *finishes his monologue.*): Citizen Juror, excuse me for bothering you. I just want to ask you something. How is ***The Prosecutor*** doing?
>
> **Juror**: Why do you want to know?
>
> **Larissa**: I just want to know if the show-trial will go on.
>
> **Juror**: Of course the show will go on! In Soviet world history, nothing's left imperfect and unfinished! In Marxist/Leninist theory, the world-historical dialectic proceeds toward its logical conclusion. Everything will be perfectly clear, at the end of history. Everything moves toward one great goal.[5]
>
> **Larissa**: Well, now, generally speaking, I guess I know all that. But in this case, I just don't know how the show-trial can go on without ***The Prosecutor*** to prosecute the case. And if that's the case....
>
> **Juror**: Why are you getting worked up, comrade citizeness? Of course, without a prosecutor, the show-trial can't go on. But that's

no big problem! That problem is easily solved! If this prosecutor isn't working, another prosecutor will pop up and pick up where the other one left off. It's just one prosecutor or another, either way or the other. Now, isn't it, citizeness? So now don't you worry. The show-trial won't just stop, because there's no prosecutor on the case. The show-trial will go on.

Larissa: Well, yes. I know that, actually, and I'm not really worried about that. I just wanted to ask you, when you decide my husband's case, please remember he's a good man, a good engineer, and a good family-man. He's my husband and he's my children's father. And....

Juror: You listen up now, lady. Why are you telling me that?

Larissa: So you'll have an idea who my husband really is, before you decide his case.

Juror: But I'm not trying anything! I am not deciding anything! I'm just a juror, understand? My role is just to sit there and pretend to be listening, and nod my head, like this. (*He demonstrates.*) And if something's said in court which I really don't understand, I just sit there and nod my head, like this....

He goes on demonstrating.

Larissa: Well, but don't you think, that among those things you don't understand, there's might be something that goes against your convictions? And then you maybe wouldn't just sit there and nod.

Juror: What's wrong with you, citizeness? Don't you understand? My convictions go along with everybody else's convictions! Because, after all, who am I, anyway? Just a juror! Just a nobody! Just a little fish in a big jury-pool. And if I don't do the job, they'll find somebody else. And nobody will know the difference. Nothing will really change. Whatever happens, happens. But, now, if you consider this case in the big world-historical perspective... Well, then I can see the whole thing with optimism. We just go along with our work, we just follow the party line, while somewhere, in our midst, there's these bestial dwarfish people. Crazy people. Stunted people. Nasty, brutish, anti-socialist people. Who do nothing but make a mess of our glorious socialist system. Because they don't go along with the party line. But someday, maybe they'll all be re-educated. They'll be rehabilitated. And someday, maybe, everything will work out right.

Larissa: Yes, maybe, someday. But what can I do for now? What can I do to defend my husband?

Juror: Nothing! You can't do anything! Because nobody really needs defending! Because everybody gets what's comin' to 'em! Ya see? And someday, everybody will see the light! Everything will come around to the big world-historical perspective. And our glorious socialist system will finally save the day, when the old state withers away, and we're living under perfect communism. In the best of all possible worlds. Don't you see? ... It might not seem like it, right now, but somehow everything works out right. It's just that everything doesn't work out right away... And, after all, these petty show-trials don't go on too much longer than two or three years, considering. And they're over before you know it, anyway.

Larissa: I'm sorry, but in this case, I can't see things the way that you do. You see things on such a grand world-historical scale. Two or three years. you say? Maybe that's nothing, to you. But I'm not a slow-witted tortoise. I can't wait that long for my husband. And my children can't wait for their father, either.

Juror: It really doesn't matter what you say, or whether you can wait or not. I'm talking about the big world-historical perspective. Where I see everything through rose-tinted glasses. (*Exits.*)

Act II, scene 3

The Second Juror *quickly walks on stage. He sees* **Larissa** *and tries to dodge the conversation.*

Larissa: Hello.

Juror (*reluctantly*): Hello. (*He tries to walk around Larissa.*)

Larissa (*blocking the way*): Excuse me. I'd just like to ask you for a favor.

Juror: Why are you bugging everybody with all your questions, lady? Maybe somebody needs to go and do something, now, and you won't let them past.

Larissa: What do you mean, somebody? You're a juror, aren't you?

Juror: Juror, schmuror. Whatever. But right now, like you can see, I'm not sitting in the jury. I'm just trying to get past you. I got better things to do.

Larissa: I know you're just trying to get somewhere, right now. But when you're sitting on the jury, you can't just avoid people who ask you for a favor. Can you?

Juror: Yeah, okay, okay. What is it you want, already?

Larissa: I only wanted to say, that my husband, Suspectnikoff....

Juror: Okay, so I know, already. Your husband's really not guilty.

Larissa: Of course he's not guilty!

Juror: But so what if he's not guilty? Everybody knows he's not guilty. I know he's not guilty, you know he's not guilty, even they (*pointing to the audience*) know he's not guilty.

Larissa (*bewildered*): But if you know he's not guilty, why are you putting him on trial?

Juror: What do you mean, why are we putting him on trial? What else would we do, if we couldn't put somebody on trial? What kind of show-trial would this be, if we didn't put somebody on trial?

Larissa: In that case, if you can't not try him, you should just acquit him. And then you could tell **The Chairman**, my husband's not guilty of anything. Couldn't you at least try?

Juror: What'll I tell **The Chairman**? That your husband's not guilty? (*Laughs loudly.*) Waddaya tryin' to do, lady? Are ya tryin' to drive me crazy? Or maybe get me killed?

Larissa: Why would I want to drive you crazy? Or get you killed, either. I just take you for a decent and clean-living man, who....

Juror: Ah-ha-ha! Ha, ha! What big words you're slinging! A decent and clean-living man! Maybe I'm not as decent and clean-living as you think, but I'm not crazy, either! (*Getting mad.*) So what you're saying, is, when they call on me, you'll get what you're asking for? Huh? You'll just show up at court, we'll admit whatever you want, and I'll do whatever you tell me to do? Is that it?

Larissa: Oh, that'd be so good of you!

Juror: Good for who? For you?

Larissa: And for you, too, maybe. If you'd just raise your voice and speak out about the injustice, don't you think it would have some political effect? It'd make the whole world a better place for everyone!

Juror: Oy veh! Speak out about the injustice! Make the world a better place! That's what they always say! And I'm sick and tired of hearing it! already. Like I really want to listen to your pitiful voice! Like I really want to blow the whistle for your stupid husband! What'd happen, is, I'd get arrested, too. And then I wouldn't be much help to you. And I wouldn't be worth a red cent to myself, either.

Throwing up his hands, he goes on muttering to himself.

Juror: Raise my voice... speak about injustice... have a political effect... make the whole world a better place! What kinds crap is that?

Larissa: Listen, what do I do, then?

Juror (*restraining himself*): You? What do you do?

Remembering the situation, he puts his hands over his mouth and whispers loudly.

Juror: Scram! Split! Get away from here!
Larissa: Get away from here? But to where? And how?
Juror (*looking around*): Go wherever you want. Nobody's keeping you here. There's nothing here for you. Or for anybody else, either. The People are disgusted, the system's breaking down, and nothing's ever gonna change. Not in two hundred years, not in three hundred years. Not even in a thousand years!
Larissa: Do you really think that nothing will ever change? But if we all worked together on my husband's case....
Juror (*frowning*): Listen to me, lady. Just get away from here, as soon as you possibly can.
Larissa: But to where? And how?
Juror: Go any way you can. Go wherever you want. Get yourself a ticket for a foreign tourist excursion, hop a ride on a hot air balloon and take a long-distance flight, find yourself a foreign husband. Whatever.
Larissa (*laughing*): Listen to you, now! What fantasies you have! I can't just fly away to a foreign country! I don't have a passport! And I'm already married! So I can't get a foreign husband. I'm just trying to help the husband I already have. And if I can't get him back from wherever they send him, I'll still wait for him to come home. I'll wait for him until there's an amnesty.
Juror: Oh, boy! Just listen to her! What stupid, high-sounding words! She'll wait for him, she says! Do you know what that means? Do you? Huh, lady? It means that year after year, you'll make complaints and appeals, and listen to the radio for news about your husband. You'll stand in line at the prison gate with a package for your husband. And you'll get exactly nowhere. And even if you knew exactly where it was that he was at, you'd still be wasting away, wondering whether you'll be allowed to talk to him through the prison bars, or if you'll maybe be able to send him an old pair of nice warm socks. C.O.D., Siberia.
Larissa: Yes, I'll do all that, if my husband needs me to.
Jurors: Yeah, well, I guess he probably will need you to. But then he'll think about what you're doing and feel sorry for himself, and maybe he'll feel sorry for you, too.
Larissa: And I'll feel sorry for him. But why should he feel sorry for me?
Juror: You really don't get it? Do you? Well, let me spell it out for you! What'll happen, is, after your husband's put in prison, he'll still think

about you, maybe, for six or seven years, while he's being tortured and he's suffering. And he'll see you in his mind, like you were in your youth, still young and juicy. But after ten years or so, when he's finally released, he'll look at you again, and what he'll see is an old grey witch with sagging breasts and a flabby belly. An old grey nag.

Larissa: And you think he'll throw me away? You think that he'll just ditch me? I'd say you don't know my husband. He's a good and noble man.

Juror: Oh, yeah? That's what you think? You think he's so good and noble? How nice that is for you! And for him, too. But while you're waiting for him, you'll get old, too. You'll waste away without love, without tenderness. And he'll get cynical, too, with all his nobleness and goodness. And he'll find, when he gets out, that he's a decrepit old man, still stuck with some dried-up, withered old bag.

Larissa: Oh my god, what are you saying? You're confusing me....

Juror: So if you don't want that to happen, just get away from here!

Larissa: But how can anybody get away? What way out of here is there?

Juror: Lady, if I knew that! You'd be talking to somebody else. And we both wouldn't be here right now.

Quickly turning away, he exits.

Act II, scene 4

The Chairman *appears. Slowly, shaking his head, he walks around the stage.*

Chairman: Despite all our dedicated work in the glorious socialist cause, this whole world's still full of suffering and injustice. Some old crusty mountaineer, who lives in a Central Asian village, lives to be a hundred and fifty. And he's healthy, and he's happy, without enemies. But me now, just look at me! I'm old and sickly, already. It's a horrible injustice! And I can't even see how I got into this mess, where nobody's sickly and suffering, except me. So now here I am, with trembling hands and a shaky head, and the whole decrepit old organism's breaking down. And why? I'll tell you why! Because nature's not set up right, so that whether a man lives longer depends on whether he's important in the great world-historical scheme. In the highest positions in our glorious socialist system....

Larissa: Excuse me, please, for interrupting your soliloquy.

Chairman: And who are you?

Larissa: Larissa Suspectnikova. The wife of the defendant Suspectnikoff.
Chairman: And is that the guy who was shooting his Kalashnikoff?
Larissa: Oh, no! That's not right! He didn't shoot anybody! He never even had a gun! He was just citing Chekov, not sighting a submachine gun. And he certainly wasn't firing at you.
Chairman: Well, what was he citing him for? Bad things happen to people who say stupid things. And to people who recite them, too. Why keep repeating them? is what I say.
Larissa: I totally agree with you. But everything needs to be taken in the right perspective. And my husband really didn't want to shoot anybody. He wasn't even carrying a gun!
Chairman: Well, yes, that's all right, then. Why should they shoot at us? We're all getting old and grey, anyway. And we'll get out of your way, soon enough. A new generation's coming. A younger generation. And maybe they'll do better by you, than we did.
Larissa: Listen, is it true **The Prosecutor**'s in really bad shape?
Chairman: So who's not in bad shape, these days? Talk about **The Prosecutor**! His position's lower than mine, and I'm not so healthy, either. Everything's all mixed up. I've got enemies everywhere. And wherever I go, I'm subject to the strictest security measures, so some screaming terrorist doesn't attack me with a knife or a gun, or maybe take me hostage. Or maybe some miserable little microbe, some miniscule bacillus, that you can't even see with a microscope, might infiltrate my vital organs, gnawing away at my liver and kidneys, killing me bite by bite. And they'd never know the cause of my death. And if I die, like that, I'm such an important person, it'd be a big disaster for the whole great socialist system.
Larissa: Yes, it would be a disaster for the whole society.
Chairman: Yes, it really would. But excuse me, I need to ask you for a little favor. Lisa Teasley was somewhere around here. Do you think you could do something for me? Could you please, citizeness?
Larissa: Yes, of course I could. Especially for you.
Chairman: But I'm afraid there's people here. What if they're watching?
Larissa: You don't need to worry about them. Don't pay any attention to them! And I'll cover for you.

The Chairman *walks over to* **The Statue of Themis**, *while* **Larissa** *covers for him.*

Larissa: Listen. You'll excuse me if I ask you about an important case? But doesn't it seem to you that my husband was arrested unjustly? My husband, Sensky Suspectnikoff....

Chairman: Of course. Completely unjustly.

Larissa: I'm so glad to hear you say that!

Chairman: And so now you're going to tell me that your kidneys hurt?

Larissa: My kidneys? What about them? No, I don't think they hurt.

Chairman: There you go again. My kidneys hurt. And I ask you: Is that fair?

Larissa: Well, no. I agree. That's totally unfair. But, like they say, that's God's will. Or something....

(On second thought.)

Larissa: But excuse me, I don't really believe that.

Chairman: In this case, it's not important. But if God can make things completely unfair and unjust, what can you expect from The People?

Larissa: Yes, you're right. I agree. But that's really none of my business. And I know that somewhere in your heart, there's still a healthy feeling for all these suffering people, that wants to be satisfied. And if you're worried about your kidneys and how your life is coming to an end... Well, maybe doing something good for somebody, like my husband, would help to ease your soul, before you go.

Chairman: Oh, you shady lady! What are you talking about? Don't you realize by now, there's no such thing as the soul! There's just chemical reactions in the white corpuscles. And that's all!

Larissa: I totally agree with you. But some people say, that when you're on your death-bed, and your life passes before your eyes, and all you see is the shattering of atoms, you might still want to keep good memories, before you go wherever you go.

Chairman (*buttoning up*): What imbecility! What good memories? Who'll remember the good things that I've done in my past life? Except maybe me and you, citizeness. People are so insane, they just squeeze and ease themselves. They do whatever helps them get through the day. Just so they'll have something to remember themselves by, a few feeble memories, when they finally pass away.

Larissa: I totally agree with you, but, you know, sometimes ....

The Secretary *rushes up to* **The Chairman**.

Secretary (*to Larissa*): Excuse me, please. (*Quickly whispers something to* **The Chairman**.)

Chairman: Aha! So that's how it is! (*To **Larissa***.) It's been interesting, but I need to go. One man, it seems, will get something out of your memories. (*Exits, supported by **The Secretary***.)

Larissa (*chasing after them*): Citizen Chairman! I forgot! I wanted to ask you for a meeting with my arrested husband! I wanted to give him some warm clothes, for the Siberian tourist-hotel.

Secretary (*hurriedly coming back*): That's nothing! If ***The Prosecutor***'s dead, that's good news for you!

Larissa: No, I don't believe it. One prosecutor dies, another prosecutor picks up the case. It's really nothing to hope for. We still need to change the whole old society, or nothing will ever get better.

Act II, scene 5

The Scientist *appears.*

The Scientist (*upon entering*): The transformation of nature. That's the only worthwhile human endeavor! To dam the Siberian rivers, turn back the Yenisee, and water the vast expanse of the Astrakhan desert, so that the Karakym becomes a flowering garden. To build gigantic water-lines and pump the Baikal waters to the Balanton Lake. To break up the icy crust of the Antarctic wastes by means of directed thermonuclear explosions. To change four hundred million square kilometers of frozen wastes into flowering gardens. To reclaim the taigas, plant fruit trees in the desert, and change the deserts into flowering gardens.[6]

Larissa: I beg your pardon, please. Are you a scientist?

Scientist: Yes, I'm a scientist.

Larissa: Well, then, I think maybe you can help me. You scientists occupy all the most important positions in our great society. And you're probably very close to the most important people in the government.

Scientist: No, no, you shouldn't exaggerate. Of course I have opinions. But, naturally, the government doesn't really listen to me.

Larissa: Still, it's a good thing I met you. Maybe you can help me. You can put in a few good words for my husband.

Scientist: What's happened to your husband?

Larissa: You see, he's been arrested.

Scientist: Ah-ha, arrested! Well, what do you know! I thought it was something important.

Larissa: Yes, it's petty, but they arrested him for nothing. And maybe if you exercised your authority....

Scientist: Regrettably, I can do nothing. The government has grandiose plans, and I promote them with some kind of scientific nonsense. That's all I can do. (*Walking away.*) I really shouldn't have said that, about thermonuclear explosions. But, still, the Yenisee might be turned back to its source.... (*Exits.*)

Act II, scene 6

The Poet *walks onto the stage, dressed extremely colorfully. One half of his pants is covered with roses, the other resembles a tossed salad; his sweater is also embroidered with different flowers, and he's wearing a snow-white scarf around his neck.*

Poet (muttering to himself):
A pretty little girl
Whirls in the haze,
On her temple, a curl
Keeps laughing as she sways....

Larissa: Oh, what lovely verses! And really good rhymes, too. Haze, sways ... Very, very good!

Poet (*Stopping himself and looking at Larissa with interest. Playfully.*): Where have you been, my enchanting child?

Larissa: I'm Larissa Suspectnikova. Right now, you see, my husband's been arrested.

Poet (*warily*): Your husband? Oh, yes. Your husband. (*Checking her out, whispering.*) Well, so what? I still want you. Stay right there, now, you sweet thing. (*Tries to get away.*)

Larissa: I'm begging you. Wait a minute! You really do need to help me.

Poet: Right now I can only give you some of my sage advice. Just be patient and wait. Soon everything will change, I promise. I've got connections, upstairs, you know. And there's this one guy... I can get Scotch whisky and Levi jeans from him. And he reads Agatha Christie in the original.

Larissa: That's very nice. But I haven't got time to waste on silly little things like that. Have you heard what ***The Prosecutor*** said?

Poet: It really doesn't matter who said what to whom. I'm not interested in your trivial problems. Right now, I'm only bothered by the Chilean coup. Just listen to this, now. (*Reads in a sing-song voice.*)

> A little Chilean temptress
> With her slim brown breasts
> Gives her whole soul to be
> In Neruda's poetry.
> But one of Pinochet's gangsters
> Picks up a Winchester
> And with a shot, lays low
> Both me and Pablo....[7]

Larissa: Wonderful! Brilliant! You have such a fighting spirit! But couldn't you give your fighting spirit to some local causes? Like, maybe if you'd write something about my husband, like this: "Just today/not far away/while the world protested/Suspectnikoff was arrested..." Or something like that. I don't know, I'm not a poet. But you are. And with poetry, you can help.

Poet (*whispering*): Do you really not understand that I'm writing about things like that? Only I write in poetic stories, like Aesopian allegories. So when I write about a Chilean girl, I'm also thinking about you. And when I write about Neruda, I'm also thinking about your husband. But, you mean, you really haven't heard about Pablo Neruda? About the Pinochet coup? And about Allende?

Larissa: Sure, I've heard about that. But do you think about **The Prosecutor**? And what he's doing, right in the here and now?

Poet (*playfully*): I just mean, you see, there's something in it for you. Listen, just give me your phone number, and I'll give you a call, sometime.

Larissa (*sadly*): Unfortunately, when Senya was arrested, my phone line was disconnected.

Poet: That's just how it is! Listen, you little witch, you inspired some poetic lines. (*Quickly kissing Larissa, he walks away, composing poetry as he goes.*) "But in Chile, the prison door-keys are all rejected/And the telephone lines are all disconnected...."

Act II, scene 7

The Writer *enters, bearded and with a staff.*

Writer (*grumbling*): These city-folk think they've got problems? Their telephones are disconnected, and they think that they have problems! Why, in the good old days, country-people lived without telephones, or anything else like that. Back then, they had cows and horses to talk to. And, for amusement, when the girls got together, to pair up, you know, they didn't waste time, like that, yakking on the telephone. These days there's just too much science. Already, because of science, you'd think our Russian rivers were running backwards to Asia! And what's that called? Progress! Bah! Humbug.[8]

Larissa: Hello.

Writer: Hello.

Larissa: I think I know you. You're a writer, aren't you? And I think I've seen your picture on the cover of some popular magazine.

Writer: That's possible, I suppose. I published my novel about a kolkhoz in some magazine or another.

Larissa: Yes, I saw it there. I admit I didn't read the novel, but I saw your photograph on it. So I thought maybe you could do something to help me save my husband. Get official attention, call out to society, sound, like they say, the alarm bell.

Writer: Alarm, schmalarm! Where is it now, that alarm bell? In the good old days, if something happened on the neighbor's farm, especially if it was Sunday, or some other holiday, from village to village, the church-bells rang out. They cried out to each other, singing, in the same voice. The church bells, the little church bells! Each one crying out against the other! Trotskyites, prisoners of war, and other non-Russian nationalities. Religion, they say, is the opiate of the people. But no, I don't agree with that! I don't think it's opium. I'm a good Party man, I think. But there's no opium for the people's soul in those old church bells. And now what? There's no church bells, there's no bell-ringers, only tractors. Like lice, you see, forgive me, that creep along with little snorts. Snort, snort, snort! Crushing the good green earth, tearing up the bowels of the soil! Ach! I hear them now! The little church-bells ringing.

Hopelessly throwing up his hands, he tries to walk away.

Larissa: Wait a minute, now. I just want to ask you something. I'm asking you to plead for my husband.

Writer: Is it Suspectnikoff, that one?

Larissa: How do you know about him?

Writer: What do you mean, know? I just sit here, watching the city-people make up things....

Larissa: That means you've seen everything, you don't need anything explained. Help him, please! I beg you!

Writer: All you people who live in cities are very strange. But how can I possibly help you? After all, I don't know anything about your city-affairs. I live in the country, far away from cities. I just sit there in the hayloft, scribbling away with my old feather-pen, like some scrawny old rooster. But every now and then, I make a business trip to Moscow. I go to Paris, London, Koctabel, Pitsundy. And then I come home again, to the village, to the chicken coop. And I go to work again. I need to work, you see, on my great masterpiece about the socialist revolution. I don't need to make your husband's case for you.

Larissa: But you're a writer. You're the conscience of the people. Nekrassov, you know, said: "You may not be a poet/But you're a citizen, and you know it!"

Writer: Oh yes, of course, I know and observe those maxims of our great classic writers. And so I stay away from the trivial cases, to address the more important, eternal struggles. The way Yesenin carried on the struggle to save the midges of the taiga.[9]

Larissa: Who? What struggle? To save what from whom?

Writer: The midges. The little gnats. They're the mosquitoes, they are, of the taiga. He took on your scientists, your geologists, your city-dwellers, who'd come to wage war against the midges. They'd exterminate them with chemicals, spraying them from a plane, like the scientists always do. But they don't stop to consider, that without the midges, nature can't exist. And we can't exist, either. I published an article about it in the Literary Gazette. Have you read it, citizeness?

Larissa (*guiltily*): No, somehow, I must 've missed it. I confess.

Writer: There, you see how you are. You don't read novels. You don't read articles. But you can't forget about Suspectnikoff, for one minute.

He tries to make a quick exit.

Larissa: Wait. I'll read your articles. I promise you. I'll read all of them. And your novels, too. Just help me, please, to get my husband released.

Writer (*coming back*): Listen, do you believe in God?

Larissa: God? I really don't know. I haven't seen him around, anywhere. But you just said that religion is an opiate of the People.

Writer: It is, of course, an opiate. But people use opium for some reason. You need some moral support. When I was young, I wanted to become a communist. But the cross is a burden on you. They don't mix with each other, the cross and the hammer-and-sickle. Especially since, in our time, everything's become godless. And all these scientific inventions, satellites and power-stations, are really good for nothing. Because they're created from nothing, they're good for nothing. Even trees are good for something in God's creation. They soak up carbon dioxide gas and make oxygen for us to breathe. (*Exits.*)

Larissa (*walking to the proscenium*): You know, I won't get anything out of them. They're all too busy saving themselves. This guy wants to save the mosquitoes. But Suspectnikoff, he cannot save. If I was a believer, maybe that might help. Because I'd say, God help us! And maybe he would. But if people don't help each other, what did he create them for? Just so they could soak up oxygen? And emit a little gas? Why do mosquitoes sting us? Why do trees breathe for us? Help us, Lord, God! Help ourselves.

The stage-lights are extinguished. The footlights flash. A deafening clap of thunder rings out. And again there is the sound of sirens, the hissing of tires, and a frighteningly bright flashing of police-lights. The stage is lit up again. **The Secretary** *comes excitedly rushing on stage.*

Secretary (*triumphantly*): Have you heard? **The Prosecutor**'s dead!
Larissa: Don't tell me! It can't be true!
Secretary: Dead, dead! I'm telling you! Dropped dead! Just like that!
Larissa: Oh, what a lucky day! What a happy day! Come here, I want to give you a kiss!

She embraces **The Secretary**, *crying and laughing at the same time.*

Larissa: Thank you! Thank you! Let me kiss you again!
Secretary (*embarrassed*): What's with you, lady! What do you think you're doing? I'm just glad to be able to bring you the good news, is all....
Larissa: But now everything will be all right. Now there'll be an amnesty and my Senya will be freed.
Secretary (*freeing himself from her embrace*): You know, I don't really know. But I don't think so.
Larissa: What? You don't think so? Why don't you?
Secretary: I just don't know, lady. I really don't. (*Exits.*)
Larissa (*alone*): Will nothing ever change?
Secretary (*coming back on stage, he strikes the palm of his hand*): That's nothing! It's good for you! But when **The Chairman** dies, everything really will get better.

Act II, scene 8

*The stage darkens. Windy sounds are heard approaching from the orchestra pit. They are performing Chopin's funeral march. The stage brightens again. The setting is a crematorium. In the background are the same old wall portraits, but now one of them—**The Prosecutor**'s—is framed with black mourning bands. The **Chairman** appears with black mourning bands on his sleeves. After him, **Gorelkin**, **The Poet**, **Greenskaya**, and **Terrorekin** came bearing wreathes. After them, **The Jurors**, **The Public Defender**, and **The Secretary** appear as pallbearers carrying the coffin, on which is written, in big red letters: **THE PROSECUTOR**. **Larissa** follows the coffin, and after her, **The Stage Worker** appears with a hammer.*

> **Chairman** (*commandingly*): Well, now. Drop it right there! Carefully, carefully! Don't bend over! Do it like this....

He demonstrates. He walks to the proscenium.

> **Chairman:** See here, now you know he's really dead. Words for the funeral eulogy of the deceased will be presented by the Chairman of the Collective for Iron-&-Concrete Construction, Comrade Greyskaya.
> **Secretary** (*in passing*): Greenskaya, Comrade Chairman.
> **Chairman:** Right, Comrade Greenskaya.
> **Greenskaya** *steps forward in severe black clothes and a black shawl. She seems somehow taller and slimmer than before.*
> **Greenskaya:** Comrades. We have suffered an un-sufferable loss. The Prosecutor has left us forever. He was a keen, sensitive, considerate, and principled comrade. Many times he graced our collective, in which, if the truth were told, there was not always a wholesome atmosphere of comradely good-humor, but instead a slovenly atmosphere of muddle-headedness and idle daydreaming. Of course, there were always shortcomings, but we've stubbornly worked to purge them, and we've mostly been successful. Except for certain cases, which I won't mention. And, for that reason, we offer our humble best wishes to the deceased. Our beloved comrade, **The Prosecutor**. (*She reads solemnly and in a singsong voice.*) It may be that you're dead, but in strong hearts and bold spirits, you will live forever, a shining example for us all, a bright beacon from murky darkness to freedom and light....

*While she continues reading, **The Worker**, at a sign from **The Chairman**, nails down the coffin lid. **Greenskaya** walks slowly away. **The Chairman** gives another* sign, and the coffin's lowered into the ground. Out of an open trapdoor a cloud of smoke rises. The submachine gunners fire their weapons into the air.

> **Chairman** (*sadly*): Now you, of course, will laugh. You'll think of **The Prosecutor**'s death only for a brief, passing moment. And then he'll be forgotten. One prosecutor passes away, another prosecutor will arise, you'll say. And that's, of course, all right, as far as that goes. But even if another prosecutor comes, it's not as simple as that. **The Prosecutor** was a romantic, an idealist. And he never took bribes. He thought only of what could be dealt with, bang! bang! bang! and nothing more. Oh, no, I wouldn't even hope, to find another prosecutor, nowadays, who'd deal with things, bang! bang! bang! pow! pow! the way he did. And even if a prosecutor came along who'd deal with things, like that… Still, behind the stunning speeches, behind all the smoke and noise, he'd just be thinking about how to snatch a cozy dacha, or how to get his nephew a cushy job in the diplomatic service. But we, the Old Red Guard, the Brave Men of the Old School, are slowly passing away from the public stage. We even forget, sometimes, what's before us, and why we're here. And, by the way, why are we here? (*Thinking, he wrings his hands.*) I don't know, I really, really don't. I only know that there's a statue here. And what a statuesque gal! Dolores Ibarruri, where are you now? I don't know, but when I see her, desire springs eternal from my loins.[10]

Unbuttoning his pants, he approaches **The Statue of Themis**.

> **Secretary**: Comrade Chairman! You can't do that here! There's people here!
> **Chairman**: Oh, piffle! There's people again! Well, get rid of the people!

He turns away and walks toward the open trapdoor.

> **Chairman**: Send them to Siberia! Or something….
> **Secretary**: Comrade Chairman, you can't do that here. You need to go over there.

He shows him the water closet, but as he leads **The Chairman** *past the open trapdoor,* **The Chairman** *accidentally falls in.*

> **Secretary**: Comrade Chairman, where'd you go?

Out of the trapdoor, smoke belches, and there's the smell of something frying.

Cries: Ah! Ah! ***The Chairman***! Help!

—Switch off the juice!
  —And send help!
—He's falling!
  —He's frying!
—Fire! Fire!
  —He's dying!

*Smoke, darkness, cries. The sounds of sirens and flashing lights. The stage-lights come back on in the theater hall. The orchestra plays Chopin's funeral waltz. Decorations and wreathes are displayed. The still living members of **The Tribunal** come on stage, carrying another black-draped coffin. Written on it in red letters is: **THE CHAIRMAN**. The clear, bell-like voice of **Greenskaya** is heard, reciting a funeral elegy.*

Greenskaya: Even though he's dead, in strong hearts and bold minds, he will live forever, a bright beacon from murky darkness to freedom and light....

Act II, scene 9

Blackout. The light come back ups. The stage furniture's all still there, the portraits are all still there, but now two of them have black frames. **The Bard** *walks on stage, and, without any prolog, starts to sing a peculiar song in a strangely monotonous voice:*

—Oh, hey there! Hello, Joe!
—Say there, how's it going, bro?
—Hey, it's going pretty slow.
  But at least it's going, you know?
—Well, it's just like they say,
  —Whatever gets you through the day.
—What more can I say?
  —It's just another lovely day.
  Refrain.
  Oh, okay! See you later, hey?
  It's another lovely day.

Oh, okay! See you later, hey?
It's another lovely day.
—Oh, hey, there! What's going on?
—Nothing much? —Nothing much.
—Oh, hey, there! What's going on?
—Nothing much? —Nothing much.
—But tell me something, please.
—Tell me please, tell me please.
—How's that neighbor of yours, dear?
—Oh, he's doing pretty fair.
> But he just can't chew or hear.
> So he chokes on his dinner, dear.
> And if he doesn't pass away
> He might just live another day.
> **Refrain.**

—Okay. See ya later, hey?
It's another lovely day.
> (repeat)

—What in the world can you say,
When you just can't face another day?
—Don't go away! Mother Nature says,
And how's the weather, up your way?
> But it's raining cats and dogs
> And in the best social catalogs
> It's said the judge and D.A.
> Have both died today.
> **Coda**

What's the debt we all must pay?
What's the pain we all must feel?
When, someday, the man of steel
Shows he's got feet of clay.
What on earth can we expect?
When we don't know who's suspect?
What are we supposed to say?
When the old world passes away?
> **Refrain.**

—Oh, okay. See ya later, hey?
It's another lovely day....
—Oh, okay. See ya later, hey?
It's another lovely day....

Larissa *rushes on stage with an old Spidola radio in her hand.*

Larissa: Have you heard? It's fabulous news! ***The Secretary*** has been appointed ***The New Chairman***!
Bard: Yes, that's interesting. Ver-ry een-terest-ingk.
Larissa: They say he's very activist, he keeps up with all the latest fads in the West, you know, and he's already working on some re-arrangements of the court. Now the juror on the left will sit on the right, and the juror on the right will sit on the left. And everything will finally work out right.
Bard: Well, that's really great. But of course, out of all that, nothing will really change. Maybe they'll rearrange the furniture on the courtroom floor.
Larissa: You think nothing will really change? But they say ***The Secretary***'s well-educated, intelligent, and wears jeans all the time, and he speaks English almost fluently. And I've heard rumors going around that he's a really big liberal. Can ***The Chairman of the Tribunal*** be a liberal? Do you think?
Bard: Why not? I guess. Everybody who speaks English has got to be a liberal, right?
Larissa: What you're saying gets my hopes up. Now I really believe that ***The New Chairman*** will begin his term by declaring an amnesty and freeing my Senya.
Bard (*putting his finger to his lips*): Shh-h-h-h!

Act II, scene 10

Blackout. Sounds of sirens, flashing police-lights, squealing brakes. Lights. ***The New Chairman*** *bustles on stage, escorted by* ***The Jurors*** *and* ***The Public Defender***. ***The New Chairman*** *is wearing jeans, Keds and a t-shirt, on which is written, "I ♥ hamburgers!"*

Chairman (*carelessly ignoring his escorts, in a staccato voice*): Vell. Goodt. Ho-kay. Nay-ver mindt. (*To himself.*) We need to catch up on our backlog, improve professional discipline, increase our educational work, stop corruption, and reform our court system, all with the same stalwart working-class spirit. We need to struggle against dilettantism, absenteeism, truancy and delays, alcoholism, dishonesty, thievery, bribery, and the demoralizing influence of foreign ideologies. And, of course, it's also always necessary to struggle against apathy, complacency, idleness, daydreaming, and muddle-headedness.

Larissa (*getting in the way of* **The New Chairman**): Hello, Comrade Chairman!

Chairman (*reluctantly, uncomfortably*): Hello.

Larissa: I wholeheartedly congratulate you on assuming your new position.

Chairman (*coldly*): Thanks very much, I'm sure. And what can I do for you?

Larissa: I just want to know when you'll free my husband. My children and I are heartsick and we want him back home, with us.

Chairman: But on what grounds am I supposed to free your husband? What's in it for me, do you think? What payoff would I get, if I should happen to free your husband?

Larissa (*flustered*): Please don't get mad at me. Don't just run me around. I know you've got many other duties and obligations. But, mostly, you can't forget, we're talking about a man's life. And you're so well-educated, you write and read English so well, and everybody says you're a really big liberal.

Chairman: What's that you say? People say that about me? (*Turning around.*) Go on, get away from me! (*The members of the court move away.*) Well, yeah, of course, I'm a liberal, but the other members of the court are still the same. And so I have to disguise my liberalism and not say anything to remind them that liberalism isn't the Great Soviet Way. (*To the members of the court.*) All right. You can come back now. What's happening to our glorious socialist system? Why isn't it working efficiently? Why hasn't the notorious Suspectnikoff been convicted, already?

Public Defender: I beg your pardon, Comrade Chairman, but we were all still occupied with burying our old colleague, the Comrade Chairman.

Chairman: Excuses, excuses! You had better have a good reason why you're not working. Everybody in their places! (***The Jurors** and **The Public Defender** take their positions.*) Where's Gorelkin?

The Voice of Gorelkin: I'm here!

*The hospital attendants bring in **Gorelkin** on a stretcher.*

Chairman: How are you, Gorelkin? Are you still in bad shape?

Gorelkin: Just like I was before. Always on the brink of death.

Chairman: Stop this sham! This charade! Enough of this circus! This farce! Bring the defendant here!

Gorelkin: At your service, Comrade Chairman!

Gorelkin jumps up from the stretcher and runs to the wings. The hospital attendants exit. *Gorelkin* drags the cage with **Suspectnikoff** onto the stage.

Chairman (*takes his place between* **The Jurors**, *wearily*): The case of Suspectnikoff, Senya Vladilenovitch, will now be resumed by this court. Suspectnikoff, do you agree with the new arrangements of the court?

Suspectnikoff: It's just the same to me. Left or right, right or left.

Chairman: Well, okay. If it's all the same to you, so much the worse for you.

Public Defender: Comrade Chairman, how can we proceed in the absence of **The Prosecutor**?

Chairman: If he's absent for good cause, of course we can proceed. We can proceed. Proceeding. Proceed with the proceedings... But we need to call upon our loyal communist supporters. (*To the audience.*) When we stopped proceeding, we were taking testimony from the witness, Comrade Greenskaya. Is she here?

Greenskaya (*jumping up on stage*): I'm always here! (*To the audience.*) Comrades. I've made the statement that our collective felt a sense of guilt because we displayed too much idle day-dreaming and muddle-headedness, and we slackened in our vigilance, because we welcomed into our ranks a certain suspicious somebody (who shall remain nameless) who introduced a foreign, hostile spirit among our members. I declared, at the beginning of this trial, that when the investigation of Suspectnikoff first began, we held suspicions about him that we couldn't even express among ourselves. We couldn't believe he'd really do such horrible things. The defendant, Suspectnikoff... We'd seen and heard, of course, how he always made fun of the court, and how he threatened the policeman with a gun. But we still thought, maybe, that he'd just snapped under pressure and had a nervous breakdown. But now we see it wasn't like that at all. It wasn't just a spontaneous, spasmodic, haphazard action. It was a deliberately pre-meditated action. It was the last in a long line of similar suspicious behaviors. The defendant, Suspectnikoff, first began by making hostile speeches, then he picked up a gun, then he attacked the police, and finally he tried to terrorize this tribunal, with such hostility that **The Prosecutor** and **The Chairman** simply couldn't carry on. Until finally... Oh, the horror! What happened next!... We've all seen... We make no excuses. We're just ashamed that we didn't perceive his spiteful, mean-spirited individualism. Until it was too late. And now

I think this court should purge itself and punish Suspectnikoff in the strictest and most severe way possible.

Chairman: But what's the most severe way possible? You mean, we should shoot him, maybe?

Greenskaya: Well, if the court deems it appropriate, maybe shoot him, even.

Cries from the Audience: That's not strict enough! Not strict enough!

Greenskaya: Well, okay. Maybe that's not strict enough. I really don't know. I just can't sort the whole thing out. But Suspectnikoff and I worked together for a really long time, and... I just can't....

She covers her eyes with her black shawl and rushes offstage.

Larissa (*jumping on stage. To the court*): No, you really can't do this! Your consciences won't let you shoot the father of two children for something he never even said. Or he never did. Or whatever.

Chairman: Listen, who gave you permission to take the stage, here? Stop carrying on like a demagogue! Enough, already, about your husband's children! And, as for your children, well, you should have thought of them before you came here! To this show-trial....

Greenskaya (*jumping back on stage*): If you ask me, all these people need to have their family rights taken away from them. We can't afford to let them spoil our children, like they've spoiled their own. Can we?

Chairman: Comrade Greenskaya, you've already made your appearance. I order you to leave the stage. (*To **Larissa**.*) And you, too, Suspectnikova. (*Cries out.*) Gorelkin!

Gorelkin (*rushes on stage*): At your service, Comrade Chairman!

Chairman: Clear the stage of these imposters!

Gorelkin: As good said as done! (*Shoving **Larissa** and **Greenskaya** offstage.*) They're offstage, already.

All three disappear into the wings.

Chairman: Now we'll hear the other side of this public show-trial. The floor is now given to **The Public Defender**. (*To **The Public Defender**.*) Only, please, restrain yourself. And be briefer, too, please.

Public Defender: With all due respect, I'll try, Comrade Chairman. Comrades of the court. As **The Old Prosecutor**, in his magnificent prosecution speech, already correctly said, we live in extraordinary times, when....

Chairman: Comrade Public Defender. Forget that old outmoded style. Spare us the flowery language. Just get to the gist of the matter. And just state your case simply, briefly, directly.

Public Defender (*hurriedly*): Oh, okay, I'll try again. Comrades of the court. Before judging and condemning the actions of my client, I only want to briefly outline the facts of the case, with a few words about his birth and upbringing. His childhood passed away....

Chairman: Comrade Public Defender, his childhood has passed away, already. Don't waste this court's time! Stick to the allotted time limits! And get on with it! Simply, briefly, directly.

Public Defender (*hurriedly*): Okay, good. I'll try again. Comrades of the court. To understand what might have been the motives of my client, it's necessary for us to look at the anti-socialist conditions in which he lived and worked....

Chairman: Comrade Public Defender. We don't need this bushwa, either. He worked and lived like everybody else. In the usual conditions. With the usual results. So get on with it! Curb your tongue! Restrain yourself! Be curt. Be humble. Be brief. Are you asking for leniency for your client?

Public Defender: That's exactly it. I'm asking for leniency for my client. I believe that in the depths of his soul, he deeply regrets his criminal misdeeds.

Chairman: And so now we'll ask him about that. Defendant, you've already heard **The Public Defender**'s famous last words. What do you have to say in your defense?

Suspectnikoff: After everything that's happened, I don't know what to say.

Chairman: You don't have to say anything. That's your right, not an obligation. You have the right to remain silent.

Suspectnikoff: I don't get what's happening here. I didn't think that, in our country, a perfectly innocent man could be arrested and imprisoned for nothing. And because of nothing.

Chairman: Now I have to warn you, defendant, you're engaging in propaganda. Don't digress. Just talk about yourself. Simply, briefly, curtly. And etcetera.

Suspectnikoff: What else was I talking about? Except what's happened to myself?

Chairman: You were talking about some hypothetical innocent man. Not about yourself.

Suspectnikoff: I was talking about a man who you arrested and imprisoned for nothing. Who you took away from his wife and put in an iron cage, like a wild beast. Who you put on trial....

Chairman (*getting worked up*): Defendant, we've already warned you not to slander this court! We simply won't permit it! We're being liberal with you! And you're abusing the privilege.

Suspectnikoff: Liberal! Schli-miberal! What are you doing, being liberal? Do you think you can show that you're liberal by arresting some innocent schmuck? locking him up like a wild beast? and throwing away the key? Do you call that liberal? Taking him away from his family and children, just like that? But what did you arrest him for? You don't even know! You don't even have a clue! You don't know why you've created this criminal justice system, and what the hell you're doing with it! But you go on arresting people, making them disappear, and condemning them to life or death. You think you can do what you want with them, you use them and throw them away. No man, you say, no problem. You say that what you want to build, your glorious socialist construction, can't be built without sacrifices. So you sacrifice people's families. You sacrifice people's lives. But you've forgotten what you're sacrificing them for....

Chairman: You will shut up! Immediately! Defendant! I'm taking away your right to speak in your own defense! **The Public Defender** will now speak for you.

Suspectnikoff: You take away my right to speak, because you're afraid of what I'll say.

Chairman: Defendant Suspectnikoff! I call upon your right to remain silent! I order you to shut your trap! I issue a gag order! Gorelkin! Shut him up! And remove the defendant immediately from the court!

Gorelkin *pushes the cage to the wings. On stage, two demonstrators appear, carrying placards that say:*

Suspectnikoff to the Gulag!!!!
A Dog Dies Like a Dog!!!

Chairman (*To the audience*): This court will retire to chambers before delivering our verdict.

Notes

1 Fyodor Tyutchev (1803–1873) is often considered the last of the great Russian Romantic poets, after Alexander Pushkin and Mikhail Lermontov.

2 The description of the Secretary reinforces his depiction as a member of the liberal intelligentsia, raising hopes that when he comes to power, the Soviet system will be reformed. Compare the hopes raised by Khrushchev's reforms after the death of Stalin and similar hopes raised by Andropov's succession of Brezhnev. As Rosalind J. Marsh observes, "Rumors that Andropov might be a liberal in cultural policy because of his liking for jazz and Western novels were soon scotched" when the new Soviet premier "advanced the traditional view that literature had the duty to help the party and state in its struggle for [law and] order." *Soviet Fiction since Stalin*, 20. In fact,

> Yuri Andropov significantly altered the [Soviet] regime's tolerance of dissidents, [....] Dissidents in Moscow soon discovered a new trend in the KGB's work—intimidation—and frequent arrests of people who were not identified publicly as active dissidents, but who read and circulated *samizdat*. [...] [As] a KGB officer told an activist whose apartment had just been searched, 'We've got a new leader now, and we're eliminating all *samizdat* and all the places where anti-Soviet literature is kept.

Joshua Rubenstein, *Soviet Dissidents* (Boston: Beacon Press, 1985), 329.

3 Larissa Suspectnikova's characterization here suggests that she serves in Voinovich's play as the moral exemplum of Soviet Russian womanhood, who, when her husband is arrested by the Cheka or deported to the Gulag, remains faithful to her husband and takes every possible measure to obtain his release, who stands in endless queues, carrying packages to be sent to him, and who endlessly petitions Soviet officials in hopes of hearing word of his release. Compare, for example, Nadezdha Mandelstam's role in preserving the memory of her husband, Osip Mandelstam, after his death, in a Soviet transport camp. See Mandelstam, *Hope against Hope*.

4 "To appreciate the change in Soviet life the dissidents [...] helped to effect, it is necessary to recall how arrests took place under Stalin. A person would not show up for work or return to his family in the evening. There were no protests, among his colleagues or from the West. [...] The achievements of the human rights movement [i.e. the Soviet dissident movement] deserve to be assessed against this enforced silence." Rubenstein, *Soviet Dissidents*, 308. The Soviet dissidents brought public attention to the enforced disappearances, the murders and tortures, partly through *samizdat* and partly through the Soviet dissident trials; and they instilled a new respect for civil and human rights through their "insistence on legality" (311). But as Rubenstein also observes, the Soviet regimes of Khrushchev, Brezhnev, and Andropov did not bury the legacy of Stalin with his corpse. Instead, "[t]he apparatus of control he bequeathed—the secret police, the labor camp system, the strict censorship [—was] not dismantled" (309), but persisted throughout the 1970s and 1980s; and arguably still exists in Vladimir Putin's New Russia.

5 According to Marxist/Leninist doctrine, the dialectical conflicts of class struggle and the eventual triumph of the working class are inevitable and will result in the creation of the communist worker's state. The Juror, like many Soviet citizens, sees this fatalistic view as an excuse not to get involved in the Soviet dissident trials. Voinovich satirizes the "true believer" who subscribes unquestioningly to Marxist/Leninist dogma in "The Only Correct World View," *The Anti-Soviet Soviet Union*, 307–14.

6 The Scientist displays his technocratic enthusiasm for the Soviet public works projects of the Stalinist era. The Yenisei is a Siberian river upon which many hydroelectric

dams were built to power Soviet industry. Lake Baikal, an enormous lake in Siberia, is located on a tributary of the Yenisei. The Karakum Desert, whose name literally means "black sand desert," is in Turkmenistan in Central Asia. Other details of The Scientist's monologue seem less directly relevant. Astrakhan is a major Russian city on the Volga, while Balanton is a lake in Central Europe, in the Transdanubian region of Hungary. The characterization of The Scientist here is also reminiscent of Faust in the later scenes of Goethe's *Faust, Part II.*

7   Pablo Neruda (b. Neftali Ricardo Reyes; 1904–1971) was a Chilean poet, diplomat, and politician who won the 1971 Nobel Prize for Literature. He joined the Communist Party in 1945 and was elected to the Senate but was subsequently exiled after writing a letter critical of President Gabriel Gonzalez Videla. In exile, he visited the Soviet Union, Poland, Hungary, and Mexico and returned to Chile in 1971. In 1969 he campaigned for Salvador Allende, who won but was subsequently deposed by the CIA-backed Pinochet coup in 1971. After receiving the Nobel Prize, Neruda returned to Chile and died only a few days after Allende, sparking rumors that he was assassinated and making him a *cause celebre* for the 1970s left.

8   The character of The Writer is Voinovich's satiric depiction of the Great Russian writer, like Solzhenitsyn, who opposes the Soviet regime from an essentially reactionary position and yearns for the restoration of the Orthodox Russia of the Czarist dynasties. Compare Voinovich's depiction of Solzhenitsyn as "Sima Simych Karnavalov" in *Moscow 2042.* Koktebel is a resort town in southeast Crimea, where Soviet bureaucrats often vacationed. Pitsunda is a tourist town in Abkhazia, Georgia, near the Russian border. Coincidentally, Alexander Solzhenitsyn's *One Day in the Life of Ivan Denisovich* was first read to Soviet Premier Nikita Khrushchev by his assistant, V. S. Lebedev, "at Pitsunda on the Black Sea coast, where [Khrushchev] was spending the summer holiday in 1962." See Zhores A, Medvedev, *Ten Years after Ivan Denisovich,* trans. Hilary Sternberg (New York: Knopf, 1978), 8.

9   Sergei Yesenin (1895–1925) was a Romantic poet who wrote ballads and songs of Russian country life. He also criticized the Bolshevik regime in poems like "The Stern October Denied Me." After a brief turbulent life, including four marriages, he committed suicide by hanging and slashing his wrists. It was rumored that his death was an execution by the NKVD, the Soviet secret police and predecessors of the KGB. See Marc Slonim, *Soviet Russian Literature* (New York: Oxford University Press, 1977), 11–18.

10 Dolores Ibarruri ("*La Passionaria*") was a Communist politician and Republican partisan of Basque origin during the Spanish Civil War of 1936–1939, who is known for her coining of the slogan, *No pasaran!,* during The Battle of Madrid in November 1936. After Franco's victory, she went into exile, but became general secretary of the Communist Party of Spain from 1942 to 1960. Following Franco's death in 1976, she returned to Spain and served in the Spanish Parliament. After resigning as general secretary in 1960, she became honorary president of the Spanish Communist Party until her death in 1989.

SECOND INTERMISSION

THIRD ACT

Act III, scene 1

The Bard*'s onstage with a guitar.*

    Bard (*croons*):
        The white river flows from far away
        But it's shallow, like our hearts.
        From the crumbs left on the table, we
        Pick up our small parts.
        Put them together, they're not much,
        They're nothing much apart.
        And since we start with nothing much
        We'll end where we did start.
           (*He breaks off singing.*)

You'll laugh, but it seems like **The New Chairman**'s not in order, either. He's hasn't even made a public appearance yet, and still, informed sources say, already the doctors are fighting for his life. They say he has a palpitating heart and an iron-hard constipation. Whether that's true or not, it will never be proven, but the nasty rumors spread, sometimes the most absurd rumors, crazy, nightmarish rumors, like he's already, this early in his life, showing his successful leadership and fulfilling some of his own brilliant ideas. Like about socialist justice and the liberal ideal, and so forth and so on. I'm always afraid when they start getting these brilliant ideas. Because when they start getting these ideas, that's when the troubles start. I just want to bury my head in the sand and wait until this whole show-trial's over and done with, already.

(*Sings.*)
> The white river flows from far away
> And the red willows rustle and blow.
> Our lives are dreams that last just a day,
> Like the snows, they come and go.
> The days rush by, the wild river flows,
> Our lives are already past.
> Between two dreams, we come and go.
> What's left? but love that lasts.

Larissa *appears with a radio, making terrible hisses and whistles.*

Larissa: Have you heard what's happening over there? In the West, I mean.

Bard: Have I heard what's happening where? As far as I'm concerned, nothing's happening anywhere.

Larissa: What do you mean, nothing's happening? How can you say that nothing's happening? You just have to listen to what they're saying....

She sets the radio on the floor, and the stifled noises change into the clear voice of the radio announcer.

Radio: ... And in the Western countries a wave of protest has arisen against the cruel, subhuman treatment of the well-known Soviet dissident and Western champion of human rights, Doctor Sensky Suspectnikoff. In Washington D.C., President Reagan has announced that the cruel and unusual treatment of prominent dissidents like Suspectnikoff demonstrates the failure of the Soviet Communist regime to deal, without violence and coercion, with its own domestic problems, not to mention international affairs. In Copenhagen, outraged demonstrators smashed windows at the Aeroflot terminal. In London, radical women from the environmental group, Greenpeace, held a sit-in strike. In France, leftist activists organized a *Committee in Solidarity with Suspectnikoff*, which includes six Nobel Prize winners. The *Committee in Solidarity with Suspectnikoff* then issued a special statement in their subject's defense....

Larissa (*switching off the radio*): Oh my god! What's going on now? Why all this uproar?

Bard: Did you really expect your husband's case to end without all this uproar?

Larissa: I didn't want the court to just condemn him, without a fair trial. But I'm afraid that all this uproar will make them even more annoyed with him. And the whole case will turn out even worse.
Bard: Don't you think it's bad enough, already?
Larissa: So what am I supposed to do?
Bard: You know that, in the West, they're just jealous of you, because they want to be the wife, or maybe the widow, of a famous political prisoner. But still, that's your best chance to free your husband. You play up the dissident angle. You remind the court what's happening in the West. You play up your husband's innocence, and the criminal injustice of the socialist regime. And you appeal to **The Public Defender**. They say that with **The Old Chairman** gone, he'll be able to bring up those old cases, and make a whole new appeal. And he's not a bad guy, either. He's just an old sportsman, a drinker, and a fisherman.
Larissa: And what do they say about his health?
Bard: Well, now. That's another question. They say that he suffers from thrombophlebitis, heart-pangs and muscle-spasms, and the whole spectrum of psychosomatic disorders. But it's possible that that's all just a trick for him to get what he wants. He's always dreamed of being **The Chairman**. But if he's **The New Chairman**, he can't suffer from episodes and seizures, or pretend to be un-healthy, like that.
Larissa: And do you think that he'll help me?
Bard: No, I still don't think he'll help you. But you need something to do. And besides... But, speak of the devil, here he is now.

Act III, scene 2

The Public Defender *strolls across the stage in rubber boots, with a fishing pole slung over his shoulder, whistling something cheerful and upbeat.*

Larissa: Hello, Comrade Public Defender.
Public Defender: Hello, Larissa
Larissa: Are you catching anything?
Public Defender: Not yet. So far, nothing's biting. But that doesn't really matter. In fishing, as in all cases, I'm not interested in the catching, but only in the catch. But what about you? Listening to the radio?
Larissa: Well, yeah, sometimes I listen to the radio. When I have time to spare. I listen to "For You, Women," or "Writers at the Microphone." Only official broadcasts.

Public Defender: Oh, come on now, Larissa. Stop being coy. You're just throwing up a smoke-screen. I'm a public defender. But I'm not an informer. What's on the radio now? Mostly just a lot of static?

Larissa: Oh, okay. I guess I have to trust you. Yes, mostly dissonant noises. Something about Green women, something about Nobel laureates. Something about breaking glass.

Public Defender: Yes, that's very interesting! It means we're really on their tails.

Larissa: I don't know anything about dissidents, or who's tailing whom, or what tails we're on, or whatever. But when my children ask me: "Where's daddy?" And I say: "Daddy's on a mission." They don't believe me. And then Igor says: "That's not true! Some kids at the school, they told me 'Your daddy's in jail!'" So just tell me the truth. Is it true, like they say? That **The New Chairman**'s really sick?

Public Defender: Well, now. Yes and no. It depends upon who you ask. But the rumors of his death have been greatly exaggerated. He's got a head-cold and a cough. He's got heart tremors and cancer in his bowels. And it's metastasizing into his liver. But nothing else much....

Larissa: Is that true? Like they say? I'm really am worried about him. I don't want to waste your time, but I've heard that you've been playing a pretty important role in my husband's trial. And I just want to ask you whether it's possible my husband might be freed. After all, there's so much static! So much noise! Coming from the West. But maybe my husband doesn't need anything like that to get him set free.

Public Defender: Yeah, yeah. You know that noise, it's simply awful, isn't it? And I really don't understand those people. Those Westerners. Those liberals. Well, okay, so they want to smash something. They want to smash injustice, say. Or they want to smash the State.[1] But why are they always smashing windows? And marching around in circles, and waving placards, and shouting slogans, like that?

Larissa: I totally agree with you. But I think, if you'd release my husband, all that noise would immediately stop. And they'd stop marching around in circles, and shouting slogans, and waving placards, like that....

Public Defender (*laughs*): Oh, ho! What a clever woman! But maybe you just don't understand, that if we release your husband, they'd suspect our weakness. And they'd go right on smashing things and breaking windows. But if you really want to help your husband, you'll talk to him, sweetly and calmly, and plead with him to confess to his crimes. And maybe you'll convince those Westerners, those liberals, those window-breakers, that we all—judge, prosecutor, jury, public defender and defendant—are pulling together with the whole strength of our glorious socialist system. And if he'll do that for us, we won't detain him too much longer. But only if your husband confesses.

Larissa: You'll free him?

Public Defender: Well, then, but what's the trade-off? You make a deal with us, and maybe we'll release him. It depends....

Larissa: You want me to talk to Senya? But they won't let me see him, even just for a minute.

Public Defender: Right, yes, that's usually not permitted. But, in this case, I think we could arrange it.

Larissa: But I can't speak for him. Senya, you know, he's so proud. So stubborn and so noble.

Public Defender (*moved*): Yes, my wife always says the same things about me. I know he's stubborn and proud. But you're still his wife, and you're still intimate with him. And maybe if you bring him something sweet, something tasty and juicy... Do you have something like that?

Larissa: Yeah, yeah. I've got something like that. I already brought something for him. Look here.

She pulls a blue rubber chicken out of her shopping bag.

Larissa: My mother, who always remembers the Great Depression, sent this treat for him....

Public Defender (*wrinkles his nose and steps back slightly*): Yum. Yes. A nice juicy chicken. But you have to persuade him with something. Maybe your mother can eat the chicken. But as for your husband, we've got to have something tastier than that. Something special, maybe. Listen, I'll give you a pass to the special buffet. Maybe you can find something there that'll tempt him to confess. Why don't you bring him some Polish sausage and German beer. Your husband likes sausage and beer, now doesn't he?

Larissa: Yes, of course he does. But I'm still worried about him. Senya's so stubborn, so proud....

Public Defender: I know, I know he is. And, believe me, I respect him for that. But maybe if you try to talk to him, we'll do our part to persuade him to confess.

Act III, scene 3

Blackout. **Larissa** *and* **The Public Defender** *disappear. When the lights come up, a cage has been brought onto the stage, in which* **Suspectnikoff** *sits with* **Chicksa**. **Suspectnikoff** *is eating swill, and* **Chicksa** *holds his hand through the bars of the cage, gazing into the distance.*

> **Suspectnikoff** (*pushing away the bowl*): No, I can't eat this swill! I have a stomach-ache and heartburn. And this stuff gives me gas. Couldn't they at least give a man something edible, on the last day of his life? Something tasty. Something juicy.
>
> **Chicksa** (*tauntingly*): Sure, I know, it's outrageous. Maybe you could get some shish-kabob and some Georgian wine, er somethin', from the special buffet.
>
> **Suspectnikoff**: Okay, okay, Chicksa. Go on with the jokes, already.
>
> **Chicksa**: I ain't joking, Sensky. It used ta be, I remember, back in the good old days, before they executed the schmuck, they'd ask the lucky guy for his last wishes. He'd get whatever he wanted. Ta drink a German beer and ta eat a Polish sausage, ta smoke a Havana cigar, or ta sleep with a woman. Whatever. And then they'd take 'im out the cell-door, read out the show-trial's verdict, maybe recite a prayer or somethin', blindfold him, and then… Bang, bang, bang, pow, pow. An' it's all finished. But that was the good old days, back when **The Old Chairman** was alive. Now that **The New Chairman**'s here, things is different. Ya can forget the cigar and the blindfold and go to meet yer death with yer eyes wide open.
>
> **Suspectnikoff**: Yeah, yeah. I'd like it like that. I'd refuse to be shackled or blindfolded. And I'd say something noble, like maybe… Well, I'd say something noble to them. I really would.
>
> **Chicksa**: Yeah, sure! Ya got nothing to say! Now, do ya?
>
> **Suspectnikoff**: Why would I not say something? I'd be sure to say something.
>
> **Chicksa**: Because ya don't get a chance to say nothing. Now they don't do none of that. Now they just come into your cell, and put a big black bag over yer head, and….
>
> **Suspectnikoff**: I don't, I don't, don't want to hear any more about that!

He puts his hands over his ears, but not completely covering them.

> **Chicksa**: Shame on you, Sensky Vladilenovich! Shame on you for stickin' your head in the sand, like a big fat ostrich! Ya need to face

the music like a man! Ya need to keep yer eyes wide open, right up 'til the end. That way, when they come into yer cell, an' they're carrying a big black bag, an'…

Suspectnikoff: Why a big black bag?

Chicksa: Ta put over yer head, ya big schmuck!

Suspectnikoff: I don't want any big black bag. I want to go out with my eyes wide open.

Chicksa: Aha! Now don't ya worry. They'll tell ya what ya gotta do. They'll put a big bag over yer head, they'll tie up your hands, and they'll bring ya to the death cell. And there, in the middle o' the floor, there'll be this big black hole.

Suspectnikoff: Why a big black hole?

Chicksa: For the blood, of course, ya schlemiel!

Suspectnikoff (*covering his ears*): I don't, don't want to hear it!

Chicksa: But ya really don't hear nothin'. With a black bag over your head, yer head's in a big black hole, an' ya don't see nothin'. You're like some frumpy old bag-lady, or something.

Suspectnikoff: You don't, don't, don't need to tell me about all that! I'm scared enough, already.

Suspectnikoff, *shivering with fear, huddles into a corner. A rattling noise of keys is heard.* **Gorelkin** *and* **Yurchenko** *enter, carrying big black bags. They throw themselves on* **Suspectnikoff**.

Suspectnikoff: I don't need it! I don't want it! I'm scared enough already!

Gorelkin (*to Yurchenko*): Better take good care o' that one! You can bet, he'll need it, where he's going.

Act III, scene 4

Abandoning **Suspectnikoff**, *the security policemen handcuff* **Chicksa** *and drag her away from the cage, wearing a big black bag over her head. They bring her to* **The Public Defender**, *who's sitting at a distance at a table. They take the handcuffs off and remove the black bag.*

Chicksa: Oh, my achin' bones! I'm gonna need crutches, already! Like you'd twist my hands off? I swear! (*Reporting to the* **Public Defender**.) I did everything, just like ya told me.

Public Defender: So, he talked? Now, did he?

Chicksa: Yeah, he talked, already. an' he's shakin' like a quakin' aspen leaf. He's ready for anything.
Public Defender: Good enough. Thank you for your work.
Chicksa: Glad ta be of service.
Public Defender: You're free to go now, Chicksa.
Chicksa: I'll go along with that! (*Exits.*)
Public Defender (*to* **Gorelkin**): Now call in the wife.

Gorelkin leaves and returns with Larissa. She's carrying a shopping bag.

Public Defender: Well, well, Larissa Suspectnikova! What've you brought with you? Something tasty, I guess. I hope you picked up some treats at the special buffet. For your husband, of course.
Larissa: There was some good stuff, there, I guess.
Public Defender: And it really hurts us to give that stuff away, Larissa Suspectnikova. But never mind now. You'll get a meeting with your husband. Maybe he'll look just a little nervous, after what he's been through. But don't make anything of it, and don't get too excited, or you'll scare him. Nobody said this was a health spa. And nobody says that you're here for your health, either. Okay, you can go into the cage, but you'd better put the stuff you brought in this big black bag.
Larissa: Why should I do that? I've already got a perfectly good bag.
Public Defender: That's an order, Larissa Suspectnikova. Some women with bags like that try to slip in some forbidden items. Like sometimes they hide a razor blade or arsenic in their brassieres, thinking we won't search. Wait a minute, Larissa.

They transfer the contents of the shopping bag into the big black bag.

Public Defender: There. That's good now. As you please, Larissa Pavlovna!

Act III, scene 5

*They throw the cage door open and **Larissa** enters the cage. **The Public Defender** shuts the door behind her, but he stays outside, listening. **Suspectnikoff**, not recognizing **Larissa**, sees only the big black bag, and huddles in the corner, hiding his eyes.*

Suspectnikoff (*cries*): No! No! No! I don't want that!
Larissa (*bewildered*): Senya? What's with you? It's Larissa!

Suspectnikoff: Larissa? (*Opens his eyes.*) Larissa. You're here, already. Does that mean, it's all behind us now? Does that mean... It's all over now? Everything's finished?
Larissa: Senya, what are you saying? What's over? What's finished?
Suspectnikoff: Yeah, she was right about that. It turns out, it's not so bad. And now I feel so excited! Such extraordinary lightness! (*To Larissa.*) Listen, are you really here? Did you die before me? But when they arrested me, you were still alive.
Larissa (*hugging him*): Senya, they've hurt you, you poor thing! Oh, but it doesn't matter! It's really not important. I'll make you better again. You don't know how much I've worried about you. I've been running in circles, worrying myself silly. And I've even started to smoke.

Larissa *takes out a cigarette and lights a match.*

Suspectnikoff: Oooh! Cough, cough.
Larissa: What's the matter with you, Senya?
Suspectnikoff: Why'd you light that match? The sulfur just reeks. It burns. And it makes me sick. (*A wild idea slowly dawns on him.*) Hey, listen. If it hurts, doesn't that mean I'm still alive?
Larissa: But of course you're still alive, Senya! You're not well, but you're alive.
Suspectnikoff: What horror! to be alive.
Larissa: What's so horrible, Senya? To be alive is good! To live, to breathe, to love. What could be more beautiful than that?
Suspectnikoff: It's beautiful to sit in a cage, to wolf down swill, and listen to your stomach rumble, and wait until somebody comes for you with a big black bag? Beautiful, when you think that they could come any day, and tie up your hands, and put on the blindfold, and then....

He notices the big black bag in ***Larissa****'s hands. Hysterically.*

Suspectnikoff: What are you doing with that big black bag?
Larissa: This bag? It's a package for you. It's a special treat. There's Polish sausage, German beer....
Suspectnikoff: German beer? And Polish sausage? No way! Is there still such a thing as Polish sausage in this world? I'd almost forgotten what it even smells like. Where on earth did you get it?
Larissa: **The Public Defender** gave me a permit to bring it from the special buffet. And there's also bread, cheese, and garlic. Do you want some beer?

Suspectnikoff: German beer? And Polish sausage? And you got all thar stuff at the buffet? Oh, now I get it. It's my final wish, isn't it? My last meal, before they put the big black bag over my head, and....

Larissa: **The Public Defender** also asked... But I really don't know how to say this to you, Senya. I know you're stubborn and proud. But think about me and the children.

Suspectnikoff (*gnawing on the Polish sausage*): I can't help the children anymore. And I can't help you. But I want you to tell them that their father was a decent, honest man. Just not very smart.

Larissa: What do you mean, "was," Senya? You're still alive and you can eat, and so not everything's lost. **The Public Defender** just asked, if you can't just confess to something, so that you can be tried and convicted. And then maybe they'll pardon you and release you.

Suspectnikoff: Pardon me? You mean, they won't shoot me?

Larissa: Well, of course, they won't shoot you!

Suspectnikoff: Hmm. And **The Public Defender** sent me sausage, cheese, and beer, just so I'd confess?

Larissa: Senya, I know you're stubborn and proud, but....

Suspectnikoff (*starting to laugh. He starts quietly, gets louder, becomes hysterical, and finally spits out the last words between laughs.*): For me? Sausage? And beer? Just so I'll confess? What trash!

Larissa: Senya, I really don't know why you're making such a scene.

Suspectnikoff: Of course I'm making a scene! I'm not ready to give up fighting, just for some lousy German beer and Polish sausage! But I really do want to live, so I can go on fighting.

Act III, scene 6

The Public Defender *has been listening the whole time. Now he enters the proscenium.*

Public Defender (*addressing the public*): Ladies and Gentlemen. Our show-trial is drawing to a close. Convict Suspectnikoff... (*Noises from the wings.*) Wait a minute. What's that noise?

Gorelkin *rushes on stage and whispers something in* **The Public Defender**'s *ear.*

Public Defender: There's some foreign correspondents here. It's too bad we can't stop them from observing the show-trial. Really, do we have to let them in? (*To Gorelkin.*) Let them in, then.

Two foreign correspondents with writing pads, cameras, microphones, and TV cameras enter.

Public Defender: We have open trials here, and that means anybody who wants to can observe the proceedings. Gentlemen, please! Don't make such a racket! (*a pause*) Now, then. Defendant Suspectnikoff has admitted his criminal behavior and faced up to it like a man. He's also admitted his criminal thoughts about our glorious socialist system and asked if he might have one last chance to speak to the public, to set the record straight about his criminal acts. And so, in strict accordance with our socialist humanist principles, we've agreed to give him that chance. I only ask you, ladies and gentlemen, that you observe the rules of the court. No passing messages to the defendant, or anything like that.

Act III, scene 7

The defendant's cage is dragged on stage.

Suspectnikoff (*washing down sausage with beer*): I can't believe it! Why, they never said that to me! And then they'll let me out of the cage? It's really hard to believe! How lucky I am! How terribly, awfully, insanely lucky! I'll live, breathe clear, fresh air, drink German beer, eat Polish sausage. Maybe even sometimes with Caspian sardines. Listen, Larissa, honey. Why aren't there any Caspian sardines?
Larissa: Why aren't there Caspian sardines where?
Suspectnikoff: Why, in the special buffet!
Larissa (*bewildered*): I didn't think of that.
Suspectnikoff: You tell **The Public Defender**, unless I get Caspian sardines, I won't confess.
Larissa: Okay, I'll tell him. I know, Senya, how really hard it is for you to confess. It's so unpleasant for you to have to confess to things you know are false. But to get out of the cage and go on living is worth a few unpleasant moments, isn't it? Even if some of us don't really want to hear your confessions.
Suspectnikoff: I don't give a damn about confessions! I spit on confessions!
Larissa: Maybe some of them will give you a hand, writing the confession.
Suspectnikoff: I don't give a damn about their hands! I spit on their hands!

Larissa: Maybe some of them will want to spit in your face.
Suspectnikoff: Spit in my face? Oh, how lovely! How beautiful!
Larissa: Why would that be beautiful, Senya?
Suspectnikoff: You really don't know? Then spit in my face!
Larissa: Why would I spit in your face?
Suspectnikoff: Go ahead, spit! Spit! And don't be shy!
Larissa: Oh, please, Senya. (*She spits in his face.*) There, are you happy now?
Suspectnikoff (*wiping it off*): That's beautiful! That's awesome! If I get spit in my face, it means that I exist. It means I'm still alive.

He walks up to the bars of the cage and starts declaiming.

Suspectnikoff: Suspectnikoff still lives and he will always live! He's our flag, our strength, and our secret weapon!
Larissa: I'm really glad you've decided to pluck up your courage, Senya. And you've made the decision to go on living as a dissident. Because you understand that the others, there in the West, are with you, in their spirits and hearts. And the Voice of America, and the BBC, and Radio Free Europe/Radio Liberty, from whatever country they broadcast, just keep whispering: Suspectnikoff, Suspectnikoff....
Suspectnikoff: Wait, wait. What are you saying? What Voice, what Liberty, what BBC? What are they saying about me?
Larissa: It's not much, what they say. But they say there's been a committee formed. And it's called *The Committee to Free Sensky Suspectnikoff*. And the American president....
Suspectnikoff: What's that? The American president....
Larissa: Yes, the President of the United States. Ronald Reagan.
Suspectnikoff: But what about him? What's he saying about me?
Larissa: Yes, he's saying things about you, Senya. But what about him? Who's he, anyway? I'm just delighted to be married to a man like you, Senya.
Suspectnikoff: What about me? And what about him? Who's Sensky Suspectnikoff, anyway? Listen, just wait a minute. What are you saying now? You're saying the American president talks about me?
Larissa: Well, of course, he talks about you.
Suspectnikoff: Just like that, he says, Sensky Suspectnikoff?
Larissa: Yes, just like that. Like he feels sorry for you.
Suspectnikoff: No way! The President of the United States knows there's a man called Sensky Suspectnikoff? Somewhere out there....

Larissa: So what? And you know there's a man like that Old What's-His-Name, the President of the United States of America. Ronald Reagan.

Suspectnikoff: Stupid chick! What are you saying? You know everybody in the whole wide world knows the President of the United States. He's Ronald Reagan! Everybody knows him! But he doesn't have to know anybody else. And he especially doesn't have to know me. Oh, how this lifts Suspectnikoff up! Oh, what incredible luck! The President of the United States knows Sensky Suspectnikoff!

Larissa: But, Senechka, dear. How can it be lucky, to be sitting in a cage? Waiting to be executed.

Suspectnikoff: Crazy woman! Stupid bitch! You've got a brain like a Greek walnut! If I wasn't sitting in a cage, the American president would never know that there's a man like Sensky Suspectnikoff! But now he really does know! He doesn't know those Bobs and Joes. He doesn't know those Borises and Ivos. But now he knows me. Sensky Suspectnikoff....

He grabs the big black bag, laughs at the few leftovers, and throws away the rest of the bottle of beer.

Larissa: Senya, what are you doing?

Suspectnikoff: Trash! Idiot! Cretin! What kind of a deal are they making with me? Do they think Suspectnikoff will sell his immortal soul for some Polish sausage and German beer? Or even for Caspian sardines? And sacrifice his good name? No way! Take them away! With best wishes to you all.

Act III, scene 8

*During the intermission, the cage has been moved to the proscenium. And **Larissa** has somehow mysteriously disappeared.* **The Public Defender** *is holding a press conference.*

Public Defender: As is well known from our previous broadcast, a new hysterical outcry has arisen from the West over the supposed violations of the human rights of some so-called innocent man. The person whose rights were violated, according to these reckless parties, is a certain Sensky Suspectnikoff, a seriously known criminal and a public enemy of our glorious socialist system. But Suspectnikoff has since admitted to all his criminal acts, and with his manly courage, he has condemned those actions harshly. He's asked for an opportunity to confess his mistakes before the whole world. And now, here's Suspectnikoff.

Press correspondents swarm onto the scene, pushing microphones toward the cage and setting up television cameras. A veritable blitz of flash-cameras follows.

Public Defender (*acting like a press correspondent*): Tell us, Suspectnikoff. Before your arrest, were you already possessed by this bestial hostility toward our glorious socialist system?

Suspectnikoff: I don't really know. It's hard to say, right now. Speaking frankly, I'd say that, although before my unwarranted arrest, I felt some hostility, I wasn't really aware of it, self-consciously.

Public Defender (*directing his hostility at Suspectnikoff*): But could you express for the audience out there, in more concrete terms, your unwholesome hatred toward our whole way of life, your bestial hostility toward our glorious socialist system?

Suspectnikoff: Yes, yes. Of course I could. But not exactly clearly. It's just that when I'd walk down the street and see all those slogans and placards, and those portraits there on the wall, I'd feel, you know, a certain resistance. And when I'd sit in the Parliament and listen to those boring speeches, I'd also feel a certain resistance. And when I'd see the Soviet Party Congress, playing on the black-&-white TV, and the delegates would be making such blustery, long-winded speeches, and everybody would be clapping, again I'd feel that stubborn resistance. And even when I'd try to watch hockey or figure skating on TV, even that would sometimes be somewhat unpleasant.

Public Defender (*slightly uneasily*): But now, of course, you see you were mistaken about all that?

Suspectnikoff: Yes, of course, I see I was mistaken. Now, after what I've been through, I've had time to think about it and to see just how mistaken I really, really was....

Public Defender: Go on, Suspectnikoff. Speak up! Tell us all about it! Write this down, ladies and gentlemen of the international press! Come closer, gentlemen and ladies, with those microphones, with those tape-recorders, so our radio listeners out there won't miss anything.

Suspectnikoff: And I think that, before my arrest, I was very passive. Just like everybody else. And when somebody was taken away, I always thought, "It's not my business. My business is to draw up blueprints, to sleep with sexy women, to drink beer and watch hockey on TV." And then, when I was arrested by the secret police, I looked around my cage and wondered, "Won't somebody do something for me?" But still, nothing happened. So now I see how it is. Today it's me, and tomorrow it'll be somebody else, and the day after tomorrow it'll be a somebody else.[2] We're all in this together, but each one of us, separately, just looks around, and says, "It's really not my business." And so instead of hanging together, we'll hang separately. They'll hang us one by one, until there's nobody left. And then I finally realized, it's not possible to go on living like that, is it? So I came to the decision that I needed to fight.

Public Defender: I'm warning you, Suspectnikoff! Think about what you're saying!

Cries from the Crowd: He's out of his mind, isn't he?

—He's a provocateur!
—Stop him!
—Police! Police!

Suspectnikoff (*with his voice muffled*): And I will fight to the last minute, to my last breath! They just wanted me to eat Polish sausages and drink German beer. (*He flings the black bag onstage.*) But Suspectnikoff won't sell his soul for a hunk of smelly sausage and a mug of stinky beer!

Cries from the Crowd: He's dangerous! Take him away! Get him out of here!

—Get him away from the press correspondents!
—But first just make him shut up!

The police and security agents push the cage into the background.

Suspectnikoff (*as he's dragged away, rattling the bars of the cage with his hands*): I'll go on fighting to the bitter end! It's better to die standing on your feet than to live squatting on your knees! I declare a hunger strike! Alert the American President! Tell him Suspectnikoff's dying, but he still won't surrender! Alert the British Prime Minister! Alert the German Chancellor! Alert the Japanese Emperor! The Dalai Lama! The Pope in Rome! And all the progressive people of the whole world!

Cries from the Crowd: Cut the lights!

—Call the police!

The lights are extinguished. Shrill police whistles shriek. The sound of sirens grows louder, automobile tires hum, there's the noise of struggles, blue police-lights flash. Finally, the noise dies away. And in the darkness, the clear, quiet voice of **The Bard** *is heard:*

—Why do flowers grow?—
A child wanted to know.
The little flower answered:
—Only flowers know!
—But is there any use for flowers
If they just blossom and blow?
—Of course there is!
 The little flower answered....

The Bard's *voice gradually fades out, but the orchestral accompaniment gradually gets louder. Finally, only the background music is heard.*
 The stage-lights come up. On stage, the whole cast stands, bowing their heads.

Notes

1 Cp. Voinovich's remarks on the collapse of the USSR: "I'm not for smashing the state. Everybody knows what happened in 1917. The collapse of this government would be a terrible tragedy for millions of people. For that reason I do not consider myself a dissident in the political sense." Voinovich, *Conversations in Exile*, 93.
2 Cp. Voinovich's remarks on the Sinyavski/Daniel trial:

> The event shook me. Up [un]til then, I had written rather critically of Soviet life, but at the same time I was completely loyal and apolitical. [...] Now I realized that events were happening that concerned me directly. Today Sinyavski and Daniel [were] on trial, and tomorrow they would try me for something or other or even for nothing at all.

"*Voinovich o sebe*," in *The Third Wave: Russian Literature in Emigration*, ed. O. Matich and M. Helm (Ann Arbor: Ardis, 1984): 140. Translated in Robert Porter, *Four Contemporary Russian Writers* (Oxford: Berg, 1989), 92. Voinovich's comments are reminiscent of Anna Akhmatova's remarks, as cited by Nadezdha Mandelstam:

> We never asked, on hearing about the latest arrest, "What was he arrested for?"; but we were exceptional. Most people, crazed by fear, asked this question just to give themselves a little hope. If others were arrested for some reason, then they wouldn't be arrested, because they hadn't done anything wrong. They vied with each other in thinking up ingenious reasons to justify each arrest. [...] This was why we had outlawed the question: "What was he arrested for?" "What for?" Akhmatova would cry indignantly whenever, infected by the prevailing climate, anyone of our circle asked this question. "What do you mean, what for? It's time you understood that people are arrested *for nothing!*"

Mandelstam, *Hope against Hope*, 11.

INDEX OF NAMES

Akhmatova, Anna 16, 122
Allende, Salvador 90, 105
Andropov, Andrei 8, 104
Aristophanes 9
Aristotle 9

Bek, Tatiana 16
Biermann, Wolf 72
Bolthushkina, Valentina 14
Borodin, Alexander 56
Braude, Irina 14
Braun, Eva 41
Brezhnev, Leonid 3, 6, 7, 8, 104
Brodsky, Joseph 7, 73

Chandler, Robert 73
Chekhov, Anton 26, 31, 68, 72, 86
Chernyshevsky, Nikolai 74
Chopin, Frédéric 94
Christie, Agatha 89
Corten, Irina H. 72, 74, 75
Crowe, Barry 73, 75

Dalai Lama, The 121
Daniel, Yuri 4, 8
Davidov, Viktor 14, 15
DeSanctis, Marsha 17
Dylan, Bob 72

Ermolaev, Herman 73

Franco, Francisco 105
Fukuyama, Frances 1, 14

Galanskov, Yuri 7
Galich, Alexander 72

Garrand, John and Carol 74
Gessen, Masha 15
Ginzburg, Alexander 7
Glad, John 76
Goebbels, Joseph 14
Gogol, Nikolai 73
Gonzalez Videla, Gabriel 105
Gorbachev, Mikhail 7
Gorky, Maxim 59, 75
Grass, Gunter 4
Greene, Graham 4
Grossman, Vasily 6, 9, 16, 73

Hayward, Max 73
Hitler, Adolf 41
Huntington, Samuel 1, 14

Ibarruri, Dolores 95, 105
Ilf, Ilya 57, 75

Khodorkovsky, Mikhail 2
Khrushchev, Nikita 2, 3, 72, 104, 105
Koleshnichenko, Svetlana 14
Kosmodemyanskaya, Zoya 45, 73

Lapega, David 75
Lenin, Vladimir 56
Lermontov, Mikhail 103
Lipkin, Semyon 6
Lourie, Richard 16, 73

Magnitsky, Sergei 2, 14
Mandelstam, Nadezhda 16, 73, 104, 122
Marsh, Rosalind J. 16, 17, 72, 104
Mauriac, François 4
Mayakovsky, Vladimir 56–57, 59, 75

INDEX OF NAMES

Medvedyev, Zhores A. 105
Mehnert, Klaus 72
Miller, Arthur 4

Neruda, Pablo 90, 105

Okudhzava, Burlat 72

Petrov, Yevgeny 57, 75
Pinochet, Augusto 90, 105
Plato 9
Plekhanov, Georgi 54, 74
Polonskaya, Veronika 75
Porter, Robert 16, 122
Profeev, Venedikt 73
Pushkin, Alexander 104
Putin, Vladimir 1, 3, 7, 74, 104

Reagan, Ronald 108, 118–19, 121
Rubenstein, Joshua 104
Rybakov, Anatoly 73

Sakharov, Andrei 6
Schroeder, Patricia 74
Silone, Ignacio 4
Sinyavski, Andrei 4, 8, 11

Slonim, Marc 105
Socrates 10
Solzhenitsyn, Alexander 3, 9, 14, 17, 73, 74, 105
Sophocles 9
Stalin, Joseph 3, 11, 73, 104

Tendryakov, Vladimir 3, 11
Trump, Donald J. 3
Tvardovsky, Alexander 3
Tyutchev, Fyodor 78, 103

Vladimov, Georgi 73
Voinovich, Marina 14
Voinovich, Olga 14
Voinovich, Pavel 14
Vyotski, Vladimir 72

Whitney, Thomas P. 74
Willets, Harry 74

Yeltsin, Boris 1
Yesenin, Sergei 92, 105
Young, Cathy 15, 18

Zinoviev, Alexander 17